Glorious RIBBONS

Glorious RIBBONS

CHRISTINE KINGDOM

CHILTON BOOK COMPANY

RADNOR, PENNSYLVANIA

A QUARTO BOOK

Copyright © 1993 Quarto Inc.

ISBN 0-8019-8502-1
ISBN 0-8019-8485-8 (pbk)

Library of Congress Catalog Card No: 93-70530

This book was designed and produced by
Quarto Inc.
6 Blundell Street
London N7 9BH

Senior Editor Cathy Meeus
Copy Editor Christine Parsons
Senior Art Editor Penny Cobb
Designer Debbie Sumner
Assistant Designer Claire Baggaley
Illustrators Sally Launder, Jane Winton, David Kemp
Photographer Paul Forrester
Publishing Director Janet Slingsby
Art Director Moira Clinch

Typeset in Great Britain by Poole Typesetting Ltd,
Bournemouth
Manufactured by Bright Arts (Singapore) Pte Ltd.
Printed by Star Standard Industries (Pte) Ltd.,
Singapore

CONTENTS

INTRODUCTION

The very sight of a display of ribbons, glowing with wonderful rich colors and luxurious textures, is enough to fire the imagination. The range of ribbons available today is wider than it has ever been; ribbons have gone far beyond the safe and predictable, and now form a key element of floral, decorative, home furnishings, and clothes trimming crafts.

Ribbon projects made in Victorian colors can create a sumptuous, traditional look.

Bring the freshness of the garden into your home with wreaths and baskets decorated with ribbons and flowers.

The use of ribbons, however, is by no means new – there are even Old Testament references to "ribbands." In certain periods of history, ribbons were the subject of legislation – only the nobility were allowed to wear them – but by the 17th century they had become popular for everyone, and the lavish use of ribbon decorated clothing became a status symbol. Men's clothing from that period could be embellished with as much as 250 yards of ribbon.

The Victorians, too, loved to use ribbons, both on clothing and on home furnishings, and it was they who invented some of the ribbon-crafts that are enjoying such a popular revival today, such

Ribbons in jazzy colors are perfect for making furnishing trims to complement a modern home.

as ribbon embroidery and weaving. You'll find these traditional crafts in Glorious Ribbons, but you'll also find a great many more modern ideas, made possible by the technical advances in the manufacture of ribbons. You'll discover how to add style and color to flower arrangements by adding bows and loops, how to trim hats, garments, and Christmas wrappings with pretty ribbon roses or rosettes, how to make ribbon patchwork or appliqué designs for a bedspread or cushion cover, and how to use craft ribbon for a series of delightful greetings cards.

Ribbon-crafts are great fun, and quick to do – ideal for our busy lifestyles. And best of all, most of them need little or no sewing skill. Whether you are gifted with nimble fingers, or are one of those who is "all thumbs," you will find projects in the books to suit your needs – even if you have only a short time to spare for craft work.

The ribbons themselves will also suit any needs, allowing you to be as

Ribbon roses in satins and sheers are ideal for creating romantic wedding accessories and gift wraps.

individual as you like in your choice of colors and styles without sacrificing practicality.

They are available in every possible finish, color and pattern, and in widths ranging from as narrow as 1/16 in (1.5mm) to as wide as 3in (80mm). The information on the next few pages will give you some idea of the variety of ribbons at your disposal, and if you need further inspiration, visit a store and see them laid out in all their glory.

CRAFT RIBBONS

Also referred to as cut-edge or florist's ribbons, these are created by cutting large rolls of fabric lengthwise into strips of the desired width. A special finish adds crispness and keeps the fabric from fraying. Because of this finish, craft ribbons are normally not washable, but some can be dry cleaned, so check the manufacturer's instructions before using them on clothes or home furnishings.

Hand-made Christmas accessories and gifts in reds and greens provide a wonderful opportunity to use ribbon-craft skills.

WIRE-EDGED CRAFT RIBBONS

These are made by fusing a wire along the edges of cut-edge craft ribbon or by fusing wire into seams made by turning over the raw edges of the ribbon. These methods are suitable only for some relatively plain weaves.

MERROWED CRAFT RIBBON

This is made with a close satin stitch that produces a fine finished edge. Most merrowed ribbons are wired, the

Wire-edged craft ribbon

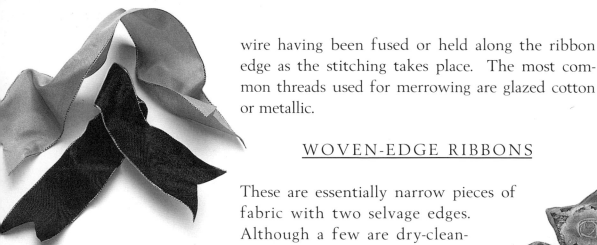

wire having been fused or held along the ribbon edge as the stitching takes place. The most common threads used for merrowing are glazed cotton or metallic.

WOVEN-EDGE RIBBONS

These are essentially narrow pieces of fabric with two selvage edges. Although a few are dry-clean-only, the majority are washable, making them ideal for any type of clothing or home furnishings project. Woven-edged ribbons are available in a wide variety of types.

Wire-edged taffeta

Grosgrain

Wire-edged woven

WIRE-EDGED WOVEN

A thin, flexible wire is woven along each edge during the manufacture. Wire-edge ribbons have exciting possibilities for shaped bows and roses, as they retain their shape indefinitely. Roses are easy to make by gathering up one of the wires like a pull-cord, and the wires can be pulled out altogether, allowing you to combine the crisp wired ribbon with soft, fluid streamers and appliquéd ribbons.

GROSGRAIN

These ribbons, which are crisp and stable, have a distinctive crosswise rib. They are available in solid colors, patterns and stripes. Stripes are generally woven in and patterns are printed on. There are some interesting variations such as a ribbon with satin edges and a grosgrain center.

SATIN

Soft, supple and easy to handle. Single face satins have one shiny and

Singleface satin

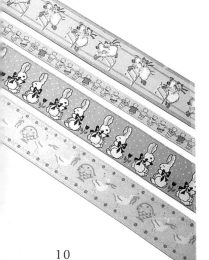

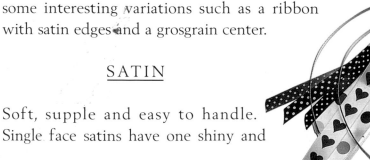

Singleface satin

one dull side, while double face are shiny on both sides and are a bit thicker than single face. Double face ribbons are almost always plain, but singleface ribbons can be printed with a pattern, generally on one side only. Special effects include picot or feather-edge, metallic edges or a grosgrain center panel with satin borders.

Moiré taffeta

Jacquards

JACQUARDS

Woven ribbons with a tapestry effect. Florals, small geometrics and ethnic patterning are the most common motifs.

TAFFETA

Very finely woven and available in both solid colors and prints, but most familiar as stripes, plaids and checks. When the design is woven in, the ribbon is the same on both sides. The overall effect of most taffetas is mat rather than shiny.

MOIRÉ TAFFETA

Crisp and elegant, with a shimmering, watermark finish, this ribbon is well suited for making bows.

Ombré taffeta

Checked taffeta

SHEER

Ideal for light, airy embellishments, such as loops and bows. Sheers can be printed or plain, and some have satin or metallic stripes woven into the sheer. Many sheers are made with a monofilament edge which is an integral part of the ribbon.

Satin-edge sheer

MONOFILAMENT-EDGE

The monofilaments are along the edges and actually function as thicker lengthwise threads that are an integral part of the ribbon's construction and cannot be removed. They are normally used for sheers or ribbons made from very fine fibers. Bows fashioned from this ribbon have a crisp appearance, but the ribbon is also soft enough to be applied to a garment.

METALLIC

Made from Lurex and similar metallic fibers, and sometimes interwoven with another fiber, these ribbons are perfect for evening wear and festive decorations. Iridescents are also used to create pearlized effects.

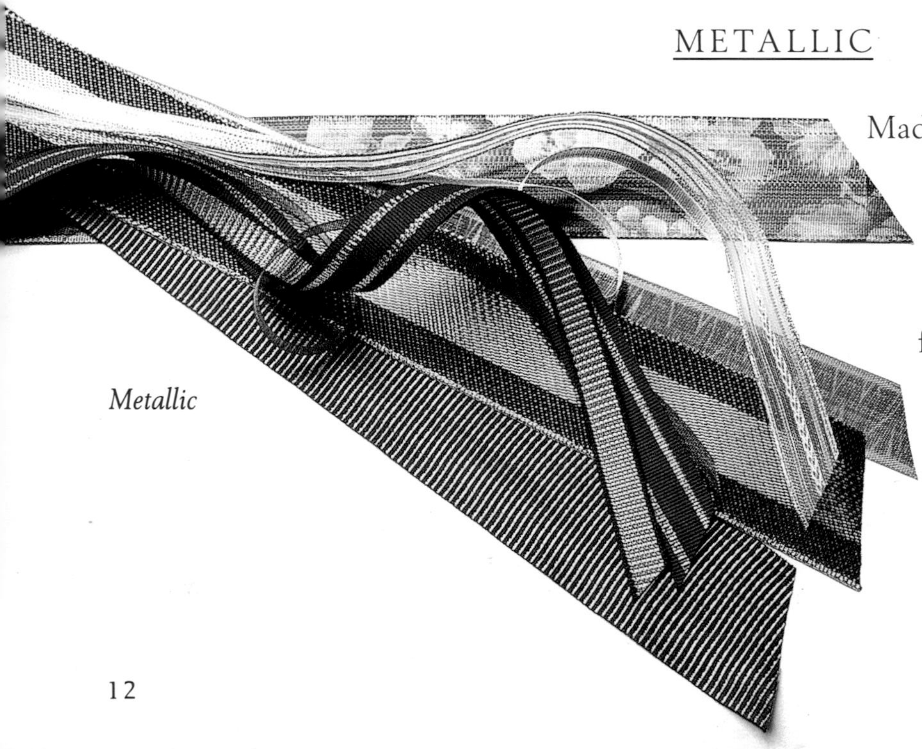

Metallic

Monofilament-edge sheer

12

VELVET

These ribbons have a plush pile, giving both deep, rich colors and solid substance.

PREGATHERED

Gathered along one edge, these are ideal for quick finishes on clothing and home decor items.

PLEATED

Knife- or box-pleated and often stitched along one edge, these can create a unique effect on both clothing and home furnishings.

EMBELLISHED

Enhanced by adding pearls or lace, embellished ribbons are popular for bridal and special occasion dressing. The base ribbon is usually, but not always, a singleface satin.

RIBBON WIDTH

Ribbons are available in a variety of widths, expressed in inches or millimeters. Consult the chart right when checking ribbon widths.

Ribbons are sold both by the yard (or meter) and in prepacked lengths. In addition, ready-made ribbon roses and bows are available in everything from sheers to satins to metallics. These can be useful, and guarantee uniform size and shape.

Velvet

CONVERSION CHART	
Ribbon Width	
1/16 in.	1.5mm
1/8 in.	3mm
3/16 in.	5mm
1/4 in.	7mm
3/8 in.	9mm
1/2 in.	12mm
5/8 in.	15mm
7/8 in.	23mm
1 1/2 in.	39mm
2 1/4 in.	56mm
3 in.	77mm

1
~

WEAVING

WEAVING TECHNIQUES • PLACE MAT AND COASTER

NECK ROLL PILLOW • WOVEN-SQUARE QUILT

WALL ORGANIZER

WEAVING TECHNIQUES

Ribbon weaving is one of the simplest needlecrafts to learn.
No special equipment or tools are necessary – most can be
found around the home or in the sewing basket.

Most ribbon weaving comprises three stages: preparing the interfacing; weaving the ribbon; and fusing the ribbon. The first and last stages are the same for all weaving. For all weaving patterns remember that the term "warp" refers to the vertical ribbons and "weft" to the horizontal ribbons.

PREPARING THE INTERFACING

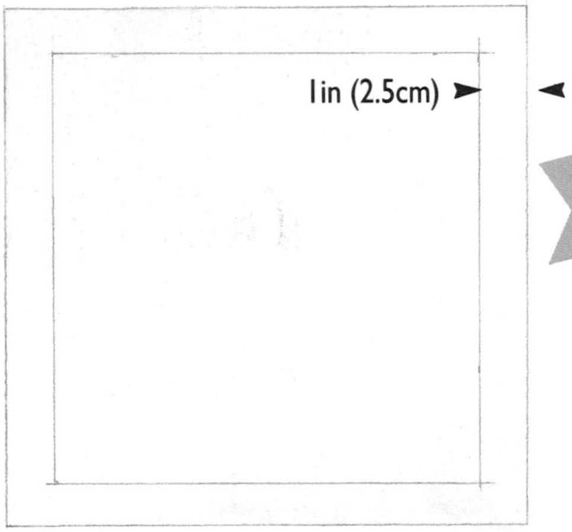

1 Draw a square of the required dimensions adding a 1in (2.5cm) seam allowance all round.
2 With the adhesive side up, pin the interfacing at its corners onto the pin board. You can now proceed with the weaving.

FUSING THE RIBBONS

1 When you have completed your weave, lightly press the ribbons to fuse them onto the interfacing, using a dry iron on a moderate setting.

Having angled the pins away from the work, you should be able to press the ribbons at the outer edge with the tip of the iron.
2 When you are sure all the ribbons are held in place, remove all the pins, turn the weaving over and with a moderately hot steam setting (or a damp cloth and moderately hot iron) press the ribbons securely in place. Allow the weaving to cool thoroughly before making it up into your chosen article.

MATERIALS

- Cork board large enough for the piece of weaving
- Glass headed pins
- Scissors
- Steam iron (or a dry iron and damp cloth)
- Light weight iron-on interfacing
- Pencil/ballpoint-pen, ruler, tape-measure
- Safety pin
- Ribbon (see Estimating ribbon quantities)

1in (2.5cm)

ESTIMATING RIBBON QUANTITIES

This chart gives the approximate quantities of ribbons needed for weaves without a diagonal weave using the same width of ribbon throughout. If you want to use different colors, divide the total length of ribbon required between the colors. The chart gives the length of ribbons required in yards (meters), including a 1in (2.5cm) seam allowance, for various sizes of woven squares.

People tend to weave with varying tensions so the quantities given above are only estimated amounts. You may find that you use a little less than those shown if you work with a loose tension.

WIDTH OF RIBBON	SIZE OF SQUARE		
	4in (10cm)	8in (20cm)	12in (30cm)
³⁄₁₆in (5mm)	6½ (6)	22 (20)	45½ (42)
¼in (7mm)	4½ (4.2)	15¾ (14.6)	32¾ (30.2)
³⁄₈in (9mm)	3½ (3.4)	12 (11)	25 (23.2)
⅝in (15mm)	2¼ (2.2)	7 (6.6)	15¼ (14)
⅞in (23mm)	1½ (1.2)	5 (4.6)	10 (9.2)

PLAIN WEAVE

To make a simple 12in (30cm) square in plain weave you will need:

5yd (4.60m) of ⅞in (23mm) ribbon in a light color

5yd (4.60m) of ⅞in (23mm) ribbon in a dark color

14in (35cm) square of interfacing

1 Prepare the interfacing as described opposite. Cut the warp (vertical) ribbons into 14in (35cm) lengths

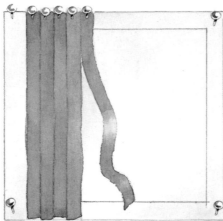

2 Pin these ribbons vertically from the top edge of the interfacing starting at the left-hand seam line. The ribbons should just be touching each other, but not overlapping. Angle the pins away from the work as this helps at the fusing stage.

Weaving is an ideal technique for making cushion covers. This cushion in soft pastel colors uses plain weave.

3 Cut the weft (horizontal) ribbon into the 14in (35cm) required lengths.

4 With a safety pin in one end, weave the first weft ribbon through the warp ribbons, over the first, under the second, over the third and so on until finally over the last ribbon. You can work either from left to right or right to left.

5 Push this first weft ribbon up to top seam line. Ensure it is straight and taut, pin it down at each end and remove the safety pin.

6 Take the second weft ribbon and weave it through the warp ribbons, this time under the first, over the second, under the third, and so on.

7 Push this ribbon up as close as possible to the first weft ribbon, ensuring it is straight and taut, then pin in position.

8 Continue weaving the remaining ribbons until you have completed all weft ribbons. Then bond the ribbons to the interfacing as described opposite.

Note You may find that your last ribbon has gone over the bottom seam line. If it is by only a small amount, do not worry as this is normal, but if it is more than ½in (1cm) either push the weft ribbons closer together, or discard the last ribbon.

ZIG-ZAG WEAVE

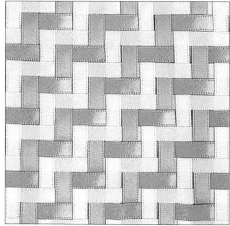

This weave works best with ribbons in just two different colors, although you can vary the effect by using different widths.

RIBBON QUANTITIES
To make a simple 12in (30cm) square in zig-zag weave you will need:

16¾yd (15.40m) of ¼in (7mm) ribbon color A

16yd (14.70m) of ¼in (7mm) ribbon color B

14in (35cm) square of interfacing

1 After preparing the interfacing as described on page 16, cut all the ribbon into 14in (35cm) lengths.

2 Starting at the left-hand seam line, pin alternate colored warp ribbons from the top edge of the interfacing. Start and finish with color A.

3 Starting at the top border drawn on the interfacing, weave the weft ribbons as follows:

ROW 1 Color A *Over 2, under 2, and so on to the end.*

ROW 2 Color B *Under 1, over 2, under 2, over 2 and so on in twos to the end.*

ROW 3 Color A *Under 2, over 2, under 2, and so on in twos to the end.*

ROW 4 Color B *Over 1, under 2, over 2, under 2, and so on in twos to the end. Repeat this sequence until you have completed your square.*

4 Fuse the ribbon weaving to the interfacing as described on page 16.

Zig-zag weave produces an immediate impact whether woven with ribbons of contrasting or coordinating colors.

PATCHWORK WEAVE

Interesting patchwork effects are easy to work and you will discover many ways of creating patchwork squares as you become more adventurous. The following design uses ribbons in three different colors.

RIBBON QUANTITIES
To make a simple 12in (30cm) square in patchwork weave you will need:

16¼yd (15m) of ¼in (7mm) ribbon color A

7½yd (7m) of ¼in (7mm) ribbon color B

7½yd (7m) of ¼in (7mm) ribbon color C

14in (35cm) square of interfacing

1 After preparing the interfacing as described on page 16, cut all the ribbon into 14in (35cm) lengths.

2 Starting at the left-hand seam line pin the warp ribbons from the

TUMBLING BLOCKS
WEAVE

top edge of the interfacing in the following sequence of colors:

ABAC/A/CABA.

Depending on the size of the piece you are working, you can add extra sequences of "ABAC" and "CABA" on each side of the central "A", which will maintain the symmetrical pattern.

3 Starting at the top seam line drawn on the interfacing, weave the weft ribbons in the same color sequence as above:

ROW 1 Color A *Under 1, and then over 2, under 2, over 2 and so on in twos.*

ROW 2 Color B *Under 1, over 1, under 1, over 1, and so on until the end.*

ROW 3 Color A *Over 2, under 2, over 2, under 2, and so on until the end.*

ROW 4 Color C *Over 1, and then under 1, over 3, under 1, over 3, under 1, over 3, and so on until the end.*

4 Repeat this sequence down to the bottom seam line. You may have a few ribbons left over.

5 Bond the ribbon weaving to the interfacing as described on page 16.

This is an exciting weave with its optical illusion enhanced by a careful choice of ribbons. It is made with the usual warp and weft ribbons plus a third narrower diagonal ribbon. The final result depends entirely on the color of the ribbons you choose.

RIBBON QUANTITIES
To make a simple 12in (30cm) square you will need:

5yd (4.60m) of ⅞in (23mm) ribbon in a light color for the warp

5yd (4.60m) of ⅞in (23mm) ribbon in a medium color for weft

8¼yd (7.60m) of ⅝in (15mm) ribbon in a dark color for the diagonal weave.

14in (35cm) square of interfacing

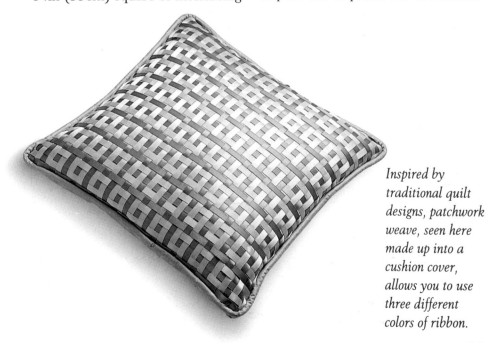

1 After preparing the interfacing as described on page 16, cut only the warp and weft ribbons into 14in (35cm) lengths – 13 of each color.

2 Starting at the left-hand seam line, pin the 13 warp ribbons from the top edge of the interfacing, with the ribbons just touching each other but not overlapping.

3 Starting at the top seam line weave the weft ribbons as follows:

ROW 1 *Under 1, then over 1, under 2, over 1, under 2 and so on to the end.*

ROW 2 *Over 1, under 2, over 1, under 2 and so on to the end.*

ROW 3 *Under 2, over 1, under 2, over 1, and so on to the end.*

Repeat this sequence for the remain-

Inspired by traditional quilt designs, patchwork weave, seen here made up into a cushion cover, allows you to use three different colors of ribbon.

ing ribbons, weaving them very closely together, touching if possible.

4 Prepare to weave the diagonal ribbon working from bottom right up through to top left. You might find it a help to use a safety pin on the end of the ribbon to feed it through.

Note: It may be necessary temporarily to remove a pin holding down a weft or warp ribbon as you thread the diagonal ribbon through, but don't forget to put it back before going on to the next diagonal.

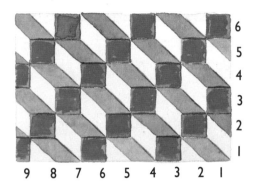

5 Begin to weave the diagonal as follows: starting from bottom right edge, feed the diagonal ribbon over the first and second warp ribbons and under the second weft ribbon. Feed the ribbon back out again from above the third weft ribbon where it crosses the fourth warp ribbon.

6 Feed the ribbon back under the fifth warp ribbon where it goes over the next weft ribbon and back out from under the next weft ribbon where it goes over the next-but-on warp.

7 Continue feeding the diagonal ribbon through the weave in this sequence until the ribbon emerges at the top left corner of the work. Pull the diagonal ribbon over the final warp and onto the seam allowance. Pin it down. Make sure the diagonal is straight and taut, then pin down the other end and cut it to length.

8 Continue weaving in the diago-

nals above the one you have just done in the following sequence: in under a weft and out from under the next weft up but two warps across. Then under the weft two above and one warp along.

9 Next, weave in the diagonals below the first one in the same way. When all the diagonal ribbons have been woven, smooth down the whole piece with your hand, repositioning some of the pins if necessary. Fuse the ribbon weaving to the interfacing as described on page 16.

Note: When weaving the Tumbling Blocks within a rectangle, the diagonal ribbons do not follow the true diagonals of the rectangle but start at one corner and eventually emerge off-set in the opposite corner.

The fresh summery fragrance of lavender captured in woven ribbon! Eleven supple lavender stems are tied together under the flowerheads with a 6ft (2m) length of ⅛in ribbon. Bend the stalks back on themselves and weave the ribbon in and out. Leave in a warm place to dry, then draw up, tighten and secure the ribbon. Trim with dried flowers and bows.

PLACE MAT AND COASTER

As these mats should be washable, choose good quality ribbons that can withstand frequent washing, and will also easily shed the occasional food or wine stain.

MATERIALS

Ribbons
- 9¼yd (8.50m) of 1½in (39mm) wide taffeta tartan
- 1¾yd (1.50m) of ⅞in (23mm) wide taffeta tartan

Other materials
- For mat: 14in by 20in (35cm by 50cm) piece of washable backing fabric, and same size in medium weight iron-on interfacing
- For coaster: 5½in (14cm) square of washable backing fabric, and same in interfacing, as above
- 3yd (2.50m) of bias binding

THE MAT

1 Following the plain weave instructions (page 17), weave a rectangle using twelve 14in (35cm) lengths of 1½in (39mm) wide ribbon as the warp and eight 20in (50cm) lengths of the 1½in (39mm) ribbon as the weft.

2 Tack the panel and backing together on right side, then round off the corners.

3 Open out one edge of the bias binding and then machine stitch it around the edges of the mat, overlapping the ends for a neat join.

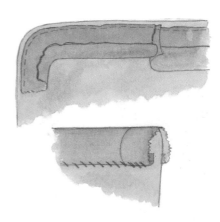

4 Turn binding to wrong side, and hand stitch edge along line of machine stitching.

THE COASTER

Make exactly as above using five 5½in (14cm) lengths of the ⅞in (23mm) ribbon for both the warp and the weft.

NECK ROLL PILLOW

This cushion uses ribbons in a variety of ways. The zig-zag weave is most prominent, with braided trims and rosettes to finish off the ends.

WEAVING

Prepare a piece of zig-zag weave 7in by 24½in (18cm by 62cm) using the 18½yd (17m) of cream and tan ¼in (7mm) wide ribbon. Trim off ribbon ends and interfacing to leave a ½in (1cm) border around the weave.

MAKING UP THE PILLOW COVER

1 From fabric cut a piece 28in by 24½in (70cm by 62cm). With right sides facing, pin, tack, and machine zig-zag the woven panel centrally across the fabric. To hide the raw edges, machine stitch a length of ⅞in (23mm) tan ribbon down each 24½in (62cm) long edge, stitching down both sides of each ribbon.

MATERIALS

Ribbons – all single faced satin
- 18½yd (17m) of ¼in (7mm) wide cream
- 18½yd (17m) of ¼in (7mm) wide tan
- 1½yd (1.20m) of ⅜in (9mm) wide featheredge cream
- 1¾yd (1.50m) of ⅜in (9mm) wide tan
- 4½yd (4m) of ¹⁄₁₆in (1.5mm) wide cream
- 7¾yd (7.10m) of ⅞in (23mm) wide tan
- 1¾yd (1.50m) of ⅛in (3mm) wide tan

Other materials
- Neck roll pillow form 18in (46cm) long and 7½in (19cm) in diameter
- Mustard cotton drill fabric 28in (70cm) square for cushion cover and rosettes
- Light weight iron-on interfacing 9in by 27in (23cm by 67cm)
- Buckram 6½in (16cm) square

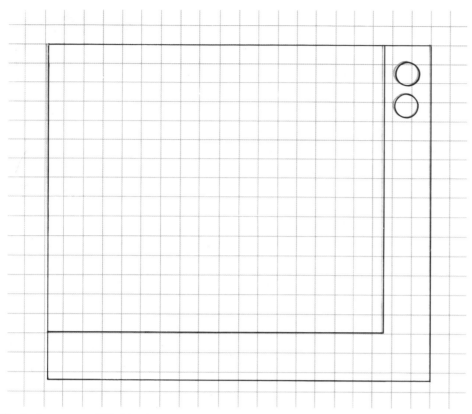

Scale 1 square = 1½in (4cm)

2 Cut the 4½yd (4m) of ⅟₁₆in (1.5mm) wide ribbon into three equal lengths and braid together as described on page 50. Cut the braid into two equal lengths, then hand sew each one to the outer edges of the ⅞in (23mm) ribbon.

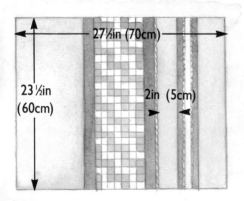

3 Approximately 2in (5cm) along from both lengths of braiding, machine stitch two rows of ⅞in (23mm) wide ribbon, butting the edges together, then machine stitch one row of ⅜in (9mm) featheredge ribbon centrally over the butted edges.

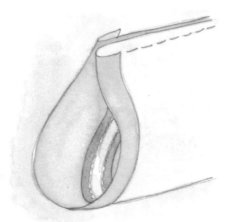

4 Right side facing, fold the fabric in half, pin, tack, and machine stitch together along the 28in (70cm) raw edge with a ½in (1.5cm) wide seam. Make a narrow casing in each end as shown, leaving a small gap in the stitching; thread a draw-string of ⅜in (9mm) plain ribbon through.

5 Insert the pillow form into the cover, pull up the draw-strings, and fasten in a bow.

THE ROSETTES

Make up two petal rosettes using the remaining ⅞in (23mm) tan ribbon, 1¾yd (1.50m) of ⅛in (3mm) ribbon, the remaining pillow fabric and two 2½in (6cm) diameter circles of buckram.

Handstitch the rosettes in place at the ends of the pillow so they can easily be unstitched and replaced before and after washing.

MAKING THE ROSETTES

1 Cover buckram with fabric to make center medallion. Turn to wrong side and stitch close to edge. Trim excess fabric.

2 Make 14 petal points from 4½in (12cm) lengths of 23mm ribbon.

3 Place in a spiral on the wrong side of the medallion as shown. Stitch or glue to secure at center.

4 Cut the ⅛in (3mm) ribbon into three equal lengths and make a simple braid (see page 50). Press and stitch around edge of medallion, folding raw edges of braid to wrong side. Stitch to secure and trim excess.

WOVEN-SQUARE QUILT

The quilt has a total of 13 plain weave squares, and uses soft, natural tones and different ribbon widths to create a very elegant effect.

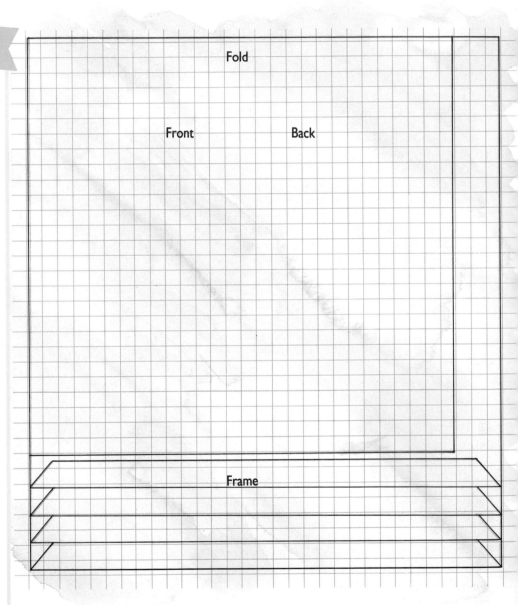

Scale 1 square = 1½in (4cm)

WEAVING THE SQUARES

Following the plain weave instructions (page 17) weave thirteen (finished size) 9in (22cm) squares. There are four different patterns.

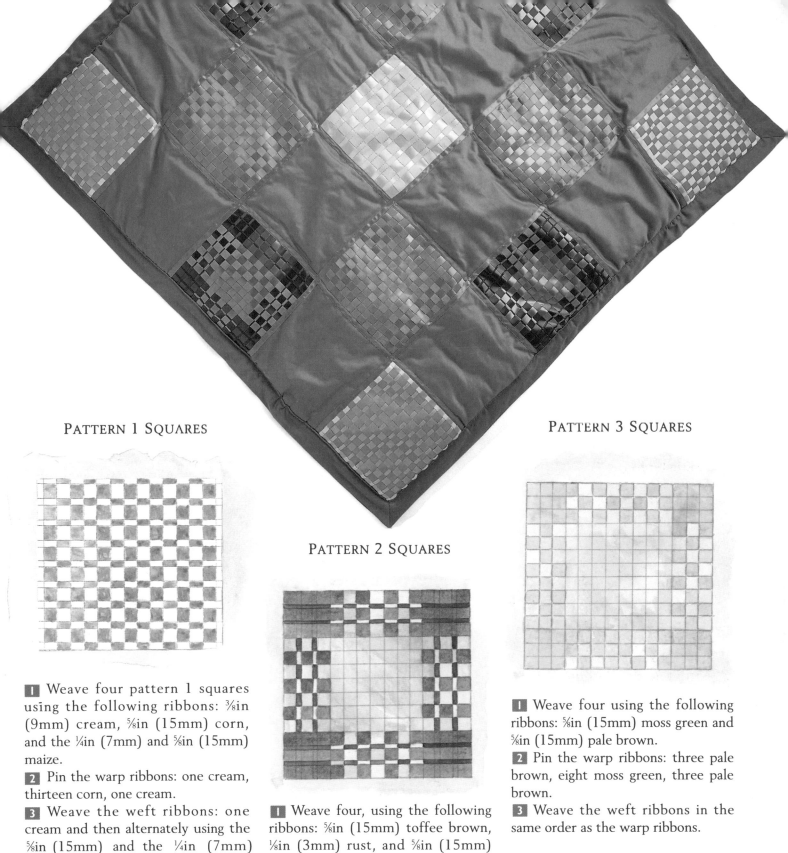

PATTERN 1 SQUARES

1 Weave four pattern 1 squares using the following ribbons: ⅜in (9mm) cream, ⅝in (15mm) corn, and the ¼in (7mm) and ⅝in (15mm) maize.

2 Pin the warp ribbons: one cream, thirteen corn, one cream.

3 Weave the weft ribbons: one cream and then alternately using the ⅝in (15mm) and the ¼in (7mm) maize and finally one cream.

PATTERN 2 SQUARES

1 Weave four, using the following ribbons: ⅝in (15mm) toffee brown, ⅛in (3mm) rust, and ⅝in (15mm) pale brown.

2 Pin the warp ribbons as follows: toffee brown, rust, toffee brown, rust, toffee brown, seven pale brown, toffee brown, rust, toffee brown, rust, toffee brown. Weave the weft ribbons in the same order.

PATTERN 3 SQUARES

1 Weave four using the following ribbons: ⅝in (15mm) moss green and ⅝in (15mm) pale brown.

2 Pin the warp ribbons: three pale brown, eight moss green, three pale brown.

3 Weave the weft ribbons in the same order as the warp ribbons.

PATTERN 4 SQUARES

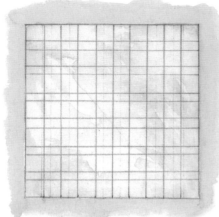

1 Weave one pattern 4 square using the following ribbons: ⅞in (23mm) stone and ⅜in (9mm) featheredge stone.

2 Pin ten of the 7⅞in (23mm) stone for the warp ribbons.

3 Weave the weft ribbons: alternately seven of the ⅞in (23mm) stone with six of the ⅜in (9mm) featheredge stone.

4 When all the squares have been completed, trim back the ribbon ends and interfacing to leave a ½in (1cm) seam allowance around each 9in (22cm) square of weaving.

MAKING UP THE QUILT

1 Cut two 50in (127cm) squares from the fabric.

2 Take one fabric square (the top) and starting 2in (5cm) in from one edge mark a further five points at 9in (22cm) intervals along the top and bottom edges and down the two sides. Using these points as guides fold the fabric across in straight lines and lightly press to form a grid to mark the positions of the woven squares.

3 Pin, tack, and machine stitch with a zig-zag the woven squares to the right side of the top fabric as shown.

4 Cut the ⅜in (9mm) toffee brown edging ribbon into eight equal lengths. Pin, tack, and machine stitch the lengths in place as shown, stitching down along both the ribbon edges to cover the raw edges of the weaving.

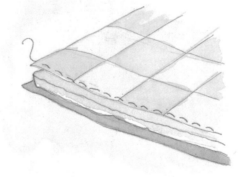

5 With wrong sides together, sandwich the batting between the top and bottom pieces of fabric. Tack together through all thicknesses around the edges.

6 From remaining fabric, cut eight strips each 54in (137cm) by 3in (7cm) for the border. Miter the ends at 45 degrees as shown.

7 Wrong sides facing, pin and machine stitch each set of four strips together across the mitered ends to form two frames. Turn to right side and trim away excess at corners.

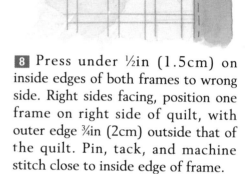

8 Press under ½in (1.5cm) on inside edges of both frames to wrong side. Right sides facing, position one frame on right side of quilt, with outer edge ¾in (2cm) outside that of the quilt. Pin, tack, and machine stitch close to inside edge of frame.

9 Place second frame on top of first, right sides together, and matching borders together at outside edges. Machine stitch a ⅜in (1cm) seam around, clip seam allowance across the corners, turn border through to right side, and handstitch inside edge of border to wrong side of quilt.

WALL ORGANIZER

Brightly colored and cleverly designed, this useful organizer is a brilliant store-all for baby's changing needs, toddler's toys, or for a teenager's bedroom.

MATERIALS

Ribbons

- 3yd (2.80m) of 1½in (39mm) wide star print
- 11½yd (10.50m) of ⅜in (9mm) wide jade
- 4yd (3.50m) of ⅜in (9mm) wide blue dot
- 3¼yd (3m) of ⅜in (9mm) wide pink
- 7½yd (6.80m) of ⅜in (9mm) wide pink dot
- 11yd (10m) of ⅜in (9mm) wide blue
- 6¼yd (5.70m) of ⅛in (3mm) wide yellow
- 4¼yd (4m) of ⅛in (3mm) wide blue
- 3yd (2.80m) of ⅛in (3mm) wide jade

Other materials

- Heavy weight interfacing 40in by 22in (100cm by 56cm)
- 3yd (2.60m) of 44in (112cm) wide blue cotton gabardine
- 24in (60cm) of 36in (90cm) wide medium weight iron-on interfacing
- 30in (75cm) length of ¾in (19mm) wooden dowel

Note In this project, medium weight iron-on interfacing is suggested for both the weaving and the stiffening of the pockets.

WEAVING

Following the instructions for plain weave (page 17), and referring to the diagram on page 29 for the position of the pockets, weave the pocket fabric.

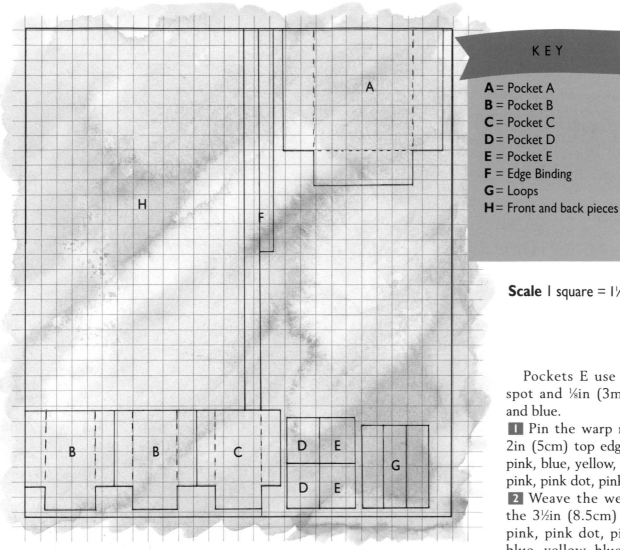

Scale I square = 1½in (4cm)

POCKET A

Plain weave 8in by 10½in (19.5cm by 27cm) using ¼in (7mm) jade and pink and ⅜in (9mm) wide blue dot ribbon.

1 Pin the warp ribbons along the 8in (19.5cm) top edge as follows: three jade, three blue dot, one pink, four jade, two pink, four jade, one pink, three blue dot, three jade.

2 Weave the warp ribbons down the 10½in (27cm) length as follows: three jade, three blue dot, one pink, four jade, four pink, four jade, one pink, three blue dot, three jade.

POCKET B

Make two pieces of plain weave 4in by 6in (10cm by 15cm) using ⅜in (9mm) pink dot and blue and ⅛in (3mm) yellow.

1 Pin the warp ribbons along the 4in (10cm) top edge: three pink dot, blue, yellow, blue, yellow, blue, three pink dot.

2 Weave the weft ribbons down the 6in (15cm) length: five pink dot, blue, yellow, blue, yellow, blue, five pink dot.

POCKET C

Plain weave 4in by 6in (10cm by 15cm) using ⅜in (9mm) blue, ¼in (7mm) jade, and ⅛in (3mm) yellow.

1 Pin the warp ribbons along the 4in (10cm) top edge: two yellow, eight blue, two yellow.

2 Weave the weft ribbons down the 6in (15cm) length: two yellow, fifteen jade, two yellow.

POCKETS D AND E

Make four pieces of basic weave each 2in by 3½in (5cm by 8.5cm). Weave two pockets D using ⅛in (3mm) yellow, blue, and jade in the weaving pattern of Pocket C.

Pockets E use ⅜in (9mm) pink spot and ⅛in (3mm) pink, yellow, and blue.

1 Pin the warp ribbons along the 2in (5cm) top edge: pink, pink dot, pink, blue, yellow, blue, yellow, blue, pink, pink dot, pink.

2 Weave the weft ribbons down the 3½in (8.5cm) length: pink dot, pink, pink dot, pink, blue, yellow, blue, yellow, blue, pink, pink dot, pink, pink dot.

When all the weaving has been completed trim off the ribbon ends and interfacing to leave just under ⅜in (1cm) border all around the interwoven shapes.

CONSTRUCTING THE POCKETS

1 Following the diagrams, draw and cut out the pocket patterns on paper and then in fabric and interfacing as follows. Each pocket has two fabric pieces, one for the outside and one for the inside. Cut out pocket A twice in fabric and once in iron-on interfacing. Cut out pockets B and C a total of six times in fabric and three in iron-on interfacing. Cut out pockets D and E eight times in fabric and four in iron-on interfacing

2 Iron the interfacing onto wrong side of outside pocket pieces.

3 Machine stitch the woven panels

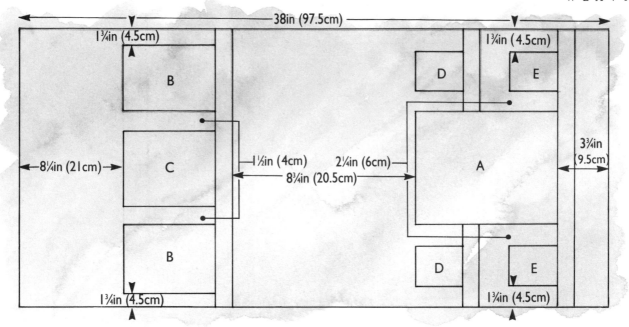

to the right sides of the pocket fronts. To cover the raw edges, machine stitch on lengths of ⅜in (9mm) blue ribbon.

4 Right sides together, seam pocket fronts and backs. Turn to right side and press.

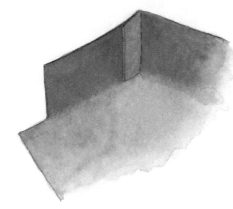

5 On inside, stitch together the right-angled lower edges of pockets A, B, and C to form a box shape.

6 Turn to right side and machine stitch close to edges.

POSITIONING THE POCKETS

1 Following diagram, draw in the positions of the pockets on the heavy weight interfacing.

2 Lay the interfacing on the fabric and cut two pieces ⅜in (1cm) larger all round for a seam allowance. Stitching around the edges, tack the interfacing to the wrong side of one piece of fabric (markings outermost). With a length of contrast-color thread, tack along all the pocket positions so they show clearly on the right side of the fabric.

3 Using this tacking as a guide, machine stitch the side edges of the small pockets D and E in place. Machine stitch the 1½in (39mm) star ribbon across the width of the organizer to cover the raw edges at the bottom edges of the pockets.

4 Turn in and press ⅜in (1cm) to wrong side on both open (bottom) edges of pocket A. Position and machine stitch this edge in place, then machine stitch side edges in place.

5 Stitch the top three pockets B and C in place in the same way as pocket A.

6 Machine stitch a length of 1½in (39mm) star ribbon just under the top three pockets.

COMPLETING THE ORGANIZER

1 With wrong sides together, tack the backing and front fabrics together, sandwiching the interfacing in between.

2 For the hanging loops cut three pieces of 1½in (39mm) star ribbon, each 9in (22cm) long. From fabric, cut three pieces 2in by 9in (6cm by 22cm). Turn in ⅜in (1cm) to wrong side down each long edge and press. Wrong sides together, lay ribbons on top and machine close to side edges. Fold each loop in half and tack in place.

3 From remaining fabric, cut two strips 40in by 1½in (100cm by 4cm) wide, and two 24in by 1½in (60cm by 4cm). Use these to bind the edges of the organizer, covering the sides first.

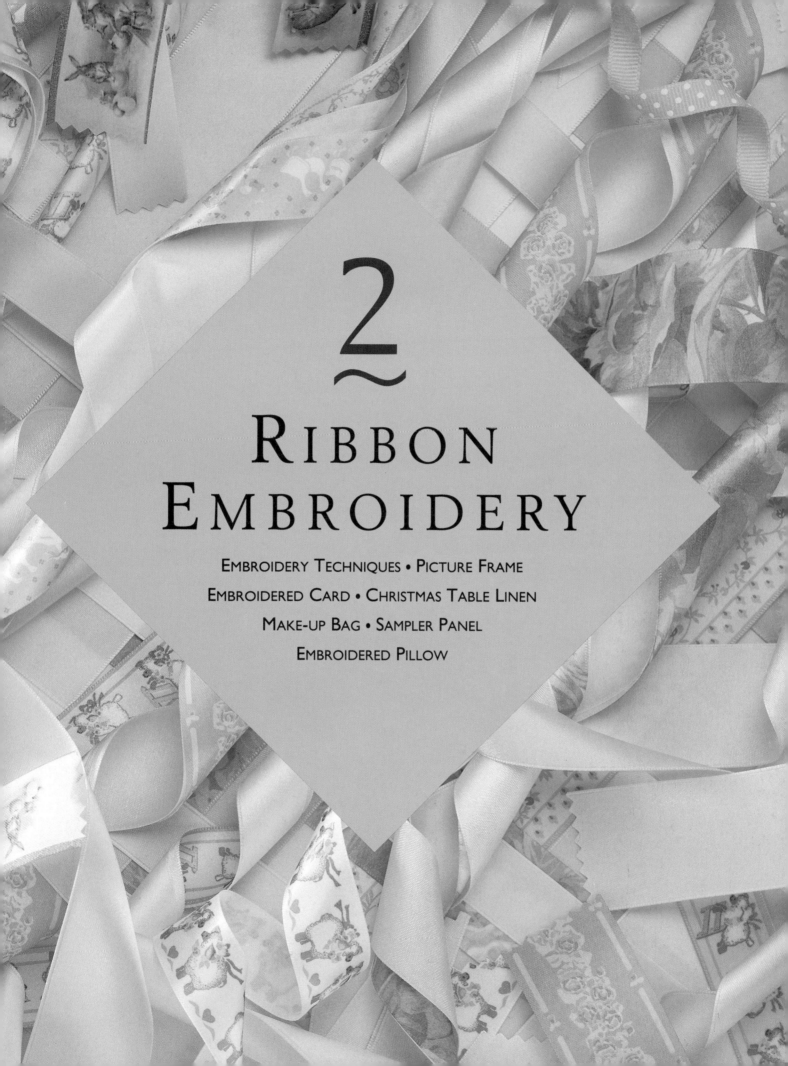

2
~

RIBBON
EMBROIDERY

EMBROIDERY TECHNIQUES • PICTURE FRAME

EMBROIDERED CARD • CHRISTMAS TABLE LINEN

MAKE-UP BAG • SAMPLER PANEL

EMBROIDERED PILLOW

EMBROIDERY TECHNIQUES

One of the oldest ribbon craft techniques, this free-style decoration uses narrow ribbons in the same way as embroidery thread.

MATERIALS AND EQUIPMENT

- Satin ribbon is the most popular choice, but other types can also be used
- Fabric, preferably fairly loosely woven. (Very fine or loosely woven fabrics may need light weight interfacing as a stabilizer)
- Tapestry needle with an eye large enough to accommodate the width of ribbon and to make a hole large enough for the ribbon to pass through the fabric
- Embroidery hoop
- Dressmaker's carbon paper
- Fabric marking pen

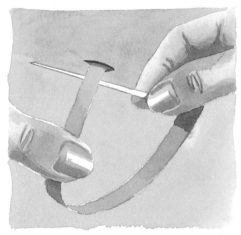

1 Hold the ribbon flat against the fabric under your left thumb while you take a stitch.

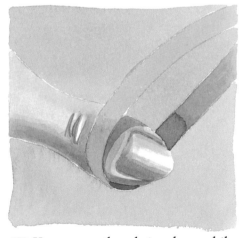

2 Keep your thumb in place while you tighten the ribbon firmly over it. In most cases this will remove twists before the stitch is completed. If you do need to adjust a stitch, carefully use a round ended tapestry needle to loosen the ribbon.

STITCHES

The projects on the following pages use a variety of stitches, each of which is illustrated here.

FEATHER STITCH

DOUBLE FEATHER STITCH

STARTING AND FINISHING

Start your first stitch by making a tiny backstitch to secure the ribbon. As a finishing stitch, knotting the ribbon creates too much bulk at the back of the work and the ribbon may come undone, so weave the ribbon behind the stitching, or leave a tail to be caught by the next stitch.

KEEPING THE RIBBON FLAT

For most kinds of embroidery it is important to keep the ribbon flat. It helps if you keep ribbon lengths short, about 12in (30cm), as it is easier to see and remove twists.

HERRINGBONE STITCH

CHAIN STITCH

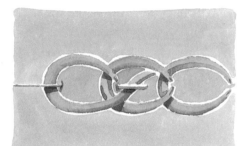

STEM STITCH

FLY STITCH

LAZY DAISY STITCH

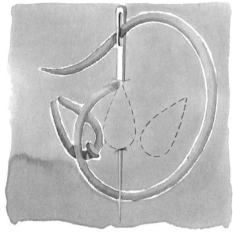

FRENCH KNOT

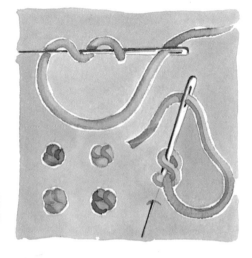

CRETAN STITCH

RUNNING STITCH

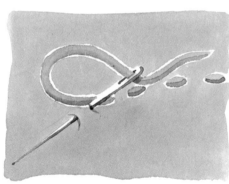

COUCHING

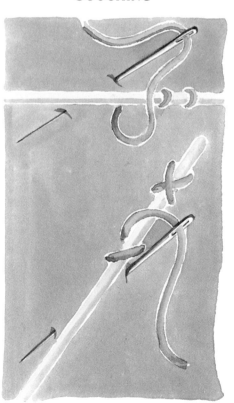

FISHBONE

BACK STITCH

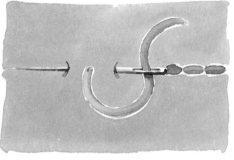

PICTURE FRAME

*Easy to make in pretty colors, this picture frame is an
ideal introduction to the art of ribbon embroidery.*

MATERIALS

Ribbons

- 1¼yd (1m) of ¹⁄₁₆in (1.5mm) wide lemon
- 20in (50cm) of ¹⁄₁₆in (1.5mm) wide dark green
- 2¼yd (2m) of ⅛in (3mm) wide mid blue
- 1¼yd (1m) of ⅛in (3mm) wide bright blue
- 1¼yd (1m) of ⅛in (3mm) wide royal blue

Other materials

- 14 count white Aida cloth 5¼in by 4½in (13cm by 11.5cm)
- Two pieces of mounting board each 4½in by 3¾in (11.5cm by 9.5cm)
- Piece of acetate 2½in by 3½in (6.5cm by 9cm)
- Fabric glue
- Clear general purpose glue

MAKING THE FRAME

1 With long tacking stitches mark out the finished size of the frame on the fabric following the measurements given.

2 Following diagram stitch the dots using French knots and the stem and leaves with five straight stitches.

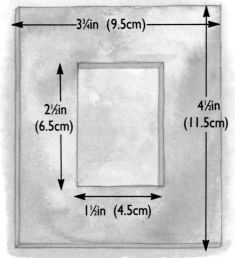

3 Cut the center from one piece of board as shown to form a frame.

KEY TO STITCHES

Blue (all shades) = French knot
Yellow = French knot
Green = Stem stitch

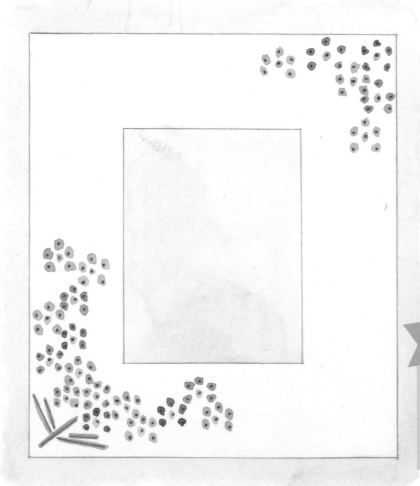

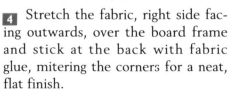

A couched trellis of narrow ribbon makes a perfect backdrop for creative floral embroidery. This Jacobean table runner features vibrant spring colors.

6 Stick the acetate to the wrong side of the frame with clear adhesive. When this is dry, stick the back mounting board to the frame on three sides with the clear glue, leaving the top edge open. Slide your photograph into this gap.

4 Stretch the fabric, right side facing outwards, over the board frame and stick at the back with fabric glue, mitering the corners for a neat, flat finish.

5 Cut out the center of the fabric as shown, clip the corners, fold allowance to back of frame, and stick in place.

7 To make a stand cut a triangle from the remaining board. Score a line ¾in (2cm) down from the top edge, bend this back, and glue it to the back of the frame.

EMBROIDERED CARD

A lasting memento of that very important day, this beautiful embroidered wedding card can be framed to display for years to come.

Ribbons

- 6 lengths of ⅞in (23mm) wide satin and taffeta in cream and white
- 12in (30cm) of ⅝in (15mm) wide cream satin
- 1¼yd (1m) of ¹⁄₁₆in (1.5mm) wide soft green satin
- 1¼yd (1m) of ¹⁄₁₆in (1.5mm) wide cream satin
- 1¼yd (1m) of ¹⁄₁₆in (1.5mm) wide white satin

Other materials

- Piece of white open-weave embroidery fabric 8in by 10in (20cm by 25cm)
- Piece of white card 8in by 10in (20cm by 25cm)
- Piece of white card 24in by 8in (60cm by 25cm)
- Sequins and beads

5 Using ¹⁄₁₆in (1.5mm) cream ribbon, stitch stephanotis on the right and left sides of the rosebud. For the flower heads on the left, make one short and three long stitches into the same hole. For those on the right, make five short stitches into the same hole.

6 Using the ¹⁄₁₆in (15mm) white ribbon, embroider lilies of the valley just below the roses with a cluster of French knots.

3 Embroider ferns using ¹⁄₁₆in (1.5mm) green ribbon, using an open fishbone stitch (see page 33). Sew loops of green ribbon among the roses to suggest foliage.

MAKING THE CARD

1 Make three stitched roses (see page 97) from the ⅞in (23mm) white ribbon and three from the cream.

4 Using ¹⁄₁₆in (1.5mm) white ribbon, stitch French knots mixed with sequins, each applied with a small bead, to suggest gypsophila.

7 Finish with trailing ribbons, folded and attached with tiny stitches along edges.

8 Pin fabric out face down, lay the 8in by 10in (20cm by 25cm) card on top, fold edges.

9 Score and fold large card into three as shown on page 110.

10 On top section only, cut out a window in the front flap 5in by 7in (12.5cm by 18cm).

11 Glue embroidery behind window, then glue first two folds of card together to finish.

2 Stitch roses to backing fabric. Fold a 2in (5cm) length of ⅝in (15mm) cream ribbon to make a flat rosebud, and stitch in place below the roses.

CHRISTMAS TABLE LINEN

Make your Christmas table extra special with this delightful tablecloth and matching napkins. Open Cretan stitch is used for Christmas garlands and wreaths.

THE EMBROIDERY

1 Draw up the motifs to size and transfer them onto the fabric corners using dressmaker's carbon paper. Note that the inner broken line is the stitch intersection point.

2 Using a tapestry needle, stitch the motif in dark green ribbon using Cretan stitch.

3 Secure loose ends by stitching them flat.

4 To finish, tie the tartan ribbon into bows (see page 82) and stitch in place.

MATERIALS

Ribbon

For each napkin motif:
- 1¼yd (1m) of ¹⁄₁₆in (1.5mm) wide dark green doubleface satin
- 12in (20cm) of ⅝in (15mm) wide tartan

For each tablecloth corner motif:
- 1½yd (1.25m) of ¹⁄₁₆in (1.5mm) wide dark green doubleface satin
- 21in (35cm) of ⅝in (15mm) wide tartan

For tablecloth centre motif:
- 4½yd (4m) of ¹⁄₁₆in (1.5mm) wide dark green doubleface satin
- 21in (35cm) of 1½in (39mm) wide tartan

Other materials
- Tablecloth and napkins in a moderately loose weave.

MAKE-UP BAG

Worked in pastel shades this versatile basket of garden flowers could also decorate a dress pocket, picture, or dressing table accessories.

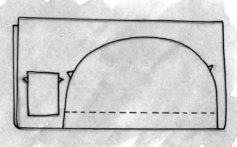

THE EMBROIDERY

1 Mark out the pieces on the fabric following the cutting diagram. Do not cut the fabric at this stage. Copy the design opposite onto tracing paper and, using dressmaker's carbon paper, transfer to the right side of the fabric.

2 Start by embroidering the basket, stitching ten vertical threads of ribbon as shown.

3 Work across with five horizontal threads weaving under one and over one, and the opposite on the way back. Couch a piece of the same ribbon along the top and base of the basket.

4 Follow the diagram and the stitch key to work the flower embroidery.

MAKING THE PURSE

1 When the embroidery is complete, cut out the fabric, lining, and batting using your traced outline as a pattern.

2 With right sides facing outwards sandwich the batting between main fabric and lining and tack together around the edge.

MATERIALS

Ribbons – all ⅛in (3mm) doubleface satin
- 2¼yd (2m) light blue
- 2¾yd (2.50m) lilac
- 2¼yd (2m) pale yellow
- 1¼yd (1m) pastel green
- 20in (50cm) pale mauve
- 20in (50cm) coral
- 20in (50cm) white

Other materials
- Main fabric 10in by 12in (25cm by 30cm)
- Lining fabric 10in by 12in (25cm by 30cm)
- Batting 10in by 12in (25cm by 30cm)
- Bias binding 35in (90cm)
- Zipper 10in (25cm)
- Pale green embroidery thread 1¼yd (1m)
- Matching sewing thread
- Dressmaker's carbon paper

Fold

3 Sew bias binding onto the top edge of each gusset piece. With wrong sides together, and matching notches and stars, join gusset pieces to sides of main pieces and machine stitch.

4 Open up zipper and machine each edge to inside of curved edges on both sides, tucking raw edges at top of zipper into seam.

5 Bind the raw ends at other end of zipper with bias binding or a small piece of left-over fabric.

6 Trim any excess batting from the seam allowance, then bind the seams in one piece, machine stitching the bias in place, then handsewing the free edge along the stitched line.

KEY TO STITCHES

1	French knot, light blue
2	French knot, lilac
3	French knot, white
4	Chain stitch, pastel green
5	Embroidery thread.
6	Pale yellow, couched with matching thread
7	Stem stitch, pale yellow
8	Five straight stitches, lilac
9	Five straight stitches, pale mauve
10	Coral stitch, pale pink
11	Stem stitch, pale green

SAMPLER PANEL

Show off your ribbon embroidery skills on a traditional sampler. It would make a charming picture to hang on the wall appropriately finished with a picture bow (see page 87).

Chart A

MATERIALS

Ribbons – All doubleface satin (DFS) unless specified as singleface satin (SFS).

- 8¾yd (8m) of ¹⁄₁₆in (1.5mm) dark green
- 4½yd (4m) of ⅛in (3mm) antique blue
- 3¼yd (3m) of ⅛in (3mm) rose
- 2¼yd (2m) of ⅛in (3mm) sand
- 20in (50cm) of ⅞in (23mm) SFS red
- 1¼yd (1m) of ⅛in (3mm) dark purple
- 1¼yd (1m) of ⅛in (3mm) wine
- 1¼yd (1m) of ⅛in (3mm) navy
- 1¼yd (1m) of ⅜in (9mm) SFS maroon
- 10in (25cm) of ⅛in (3mm) bright blue
- 20in (50cm) of ⅛in (3mm) pale brown
- 20in (50cm) of ⅛in (3mm) white
- 20in (50cm) of ¹⁄₁₆ or ⅛in (1.5 or 3mm) black

Other materials

- 14 count white Aida cloth 10½ in by 13in (26cm by 33cm)
- Hardboard (or very strong, thick card) 8¾in by 12in (22cm by 30cm)
- Pale brown sewing thread
- Buttonhole twist
- Frame 8¾in by 12in (22cm by 30cm)

The sampler measures 8¼in by 11¾in (21cm by 29.5cm) and uses the following stitches and colors:

Border Double feather stitch – dark green. French knot – antique blue and rose.

Flower Basket Ribbon weaving – sand. Flowers, full and half – red.

Friezes Outlines in herringbone stitch – dark purple, wine, rose, navy. Leaves in lazy daisy stitch – dark green. Rosebud – maroon. Roseleaf in fishbone stitch – dark green. Bellflower – bright blue.

Tree Leaves in fishbone stitch – dark green. Trunk in couching – pale brown ribbon and matching sewing thread.

House Roof and door in running stitch and back stitch – antique

blue navy. Flower stalks in fly stitch – dark green.

Sheep French knots – black, white.

THE EMBROIDERY

1 Mark the center of the fabric by folding it in half vertically and then horizontally, pressing, and then opening out. Work the central panel first from Chart A.

Chart D

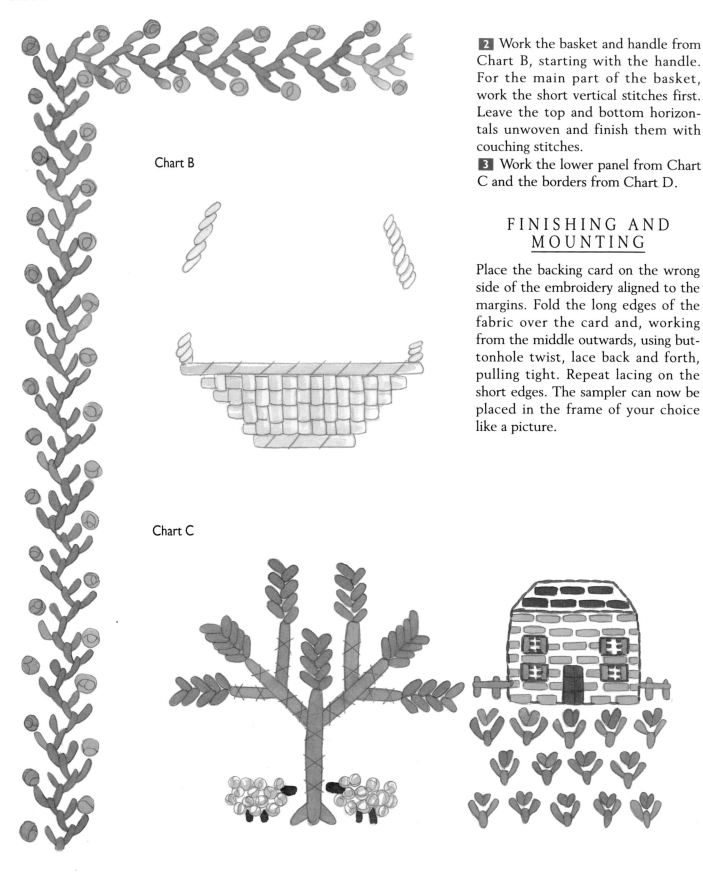

Chart B

Chart C

2 Work the basket and handle from Chart B, starting with the handle. For the main part of the basket, work the short vertical stitches first. Leave the top and bottom horizontals unwoven and finish them with couching stitches.

3 Work the lower panel from Chart C and the borders from Chart D.

FINISHING AND MOUNTING

Place the backing card on the wrong side of the embroidery aligned to the margins. Fold the long edges of the fabric over the card and, working from the middle outwards, using buttonhole twist, lace back and forth, pulling tight. Repeat lacing on the short edges. The sampler can now be placed in the frame of your choice like a picture.

EMBROIDERED PILLOW

This enchanting posy of ribbon flowers makes a perfect keepsake. The flower motif could equally well be used to decorate a pretty wedding or christening card.

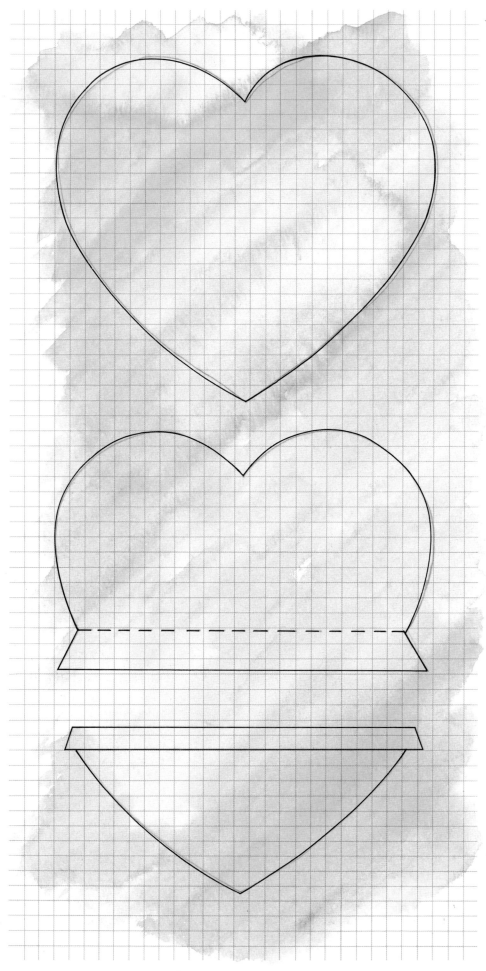

Ribbons
- 2¼yd (2m) of ¹/₁₆in (1.5mm) wide doublefaced satin in each of the following colours – soft green, rose, mauve, light pink, cream
- 8in (20cm) of ⅝in (15mm) mauve
- 16in (40cm) of ⅜in (9mm) ivory
- 16in (40cm) of ⅜in (9mm) light pink
- 16in (40cm) of ⅜in (9mm) rose

Other materials
- Pink moiré satin 12in by 45in (30cm by 115cm)
- 2¼yd (2m) cream lace
- Heart shaped pillow form
- Stitch and Tear stabilizer
- Needle with large eye
- Three snaps
- Sewing threads to match fabric and lace
- Stranded embroidery cotton in cream and soft green

PREPARING THE FABRIC

1 Make a paper pattern from the diagrams, cut out the front and the two back pillow pieces from the satin fabric.

2 Using dressmaker's carbon paper, transfer embroidery design to the right side of the front piece of satin.

3 Tack a layer of Stitch and Tear to the wrong side of the front satin piece behind the embroidery design.

THE EMBROIDERY

1 Work the ribbon and cotton embroidery for the small flowers and leaves following the stitch and color keys supplied. Use three strands of thread for the cotton embroidery. Use 16in (40cm) lengths of ribbon leaving about ¾in (2cm) of ribbon at

Scale 1 square = ⅜in (1cm)

back of work. When complete, neatly sew ends of ribbon flat using sewing thread.

2 Make a bow using pieces of ⅟₁₆in (1.5mm) wide light pink and mauve ribbon. Stitch in place at the top of green stems.

THE FLOWERS

Make flowers as follows.

MAUVE BELLFLOWER (1)

1 Take approx 2½in (6cm) of the ⅝in (15mm) wide mauve ribbon and fold raw ends to the wrong side.

2 Fold in half, stitching folded raw ends together.

3 Now bring corners towards centre, turn in raw edges and stitch to secure.

4 Make loops with three lengths of ⅟₁₆in (1.5mm) wide rose. Tuck them inside bell and stitch in place.

LIGHT PINK GATHERED FLOWERS (2)

1 Take a 4in (10cm) length of ⅜in (9mm) wide ribbon and join along short ends to make a loop.

2 Run a line of gathering stitches around ribbon circle and pull up gathers to form a flower. Fasten off thread and stitch in place.

IVORY GATHERED FLOWER (1)

1 Make a gathered flower as above using ivory ribbon.

2 Make four small loops using ⅟₁₆in (1.5mm) mauve ribbon and tuck them into the center of the flower. Stitch in place.

LOOP LEAVES (3)

For each set make three or four loops using 4in (10cm) strips of ⅟₁₆in (1.5mm) wide soft green ribbon. Stitch loops together.

ROSES

1 Make two stitched roses, one ivory and one rose, from ⅜in (9mm) ribbon as described on page 97.

KEY

1 **Soft green ribbon** couched with green stranded cotton

2 **Green stranded cotton** straight stitch

3 **Rose ribbon** lazy daisy stitch

4 **Mauve ribbon** lazy daisy stitch

5 **Light pink ribbon** lazy daisy stitch

6 **Cream ribbon** lazy daisy stitch

7 **Light pink ribbon** French knots

All lazy daisy flowers have cream stranded cotton French knot centers.

MAKING UP THE PILLOW

1 Sew a line of running stitches along edge of lace and pull up to fit edge of front pillow. With the right side of the pillow facing and matching raw edges pin and tack the lace along stitching line.

2 Turn and machine stitch ½in (1cm) to wrong side along the center edge on both back pieces. With right side facing up, pin the two back pieces together, overlapping at the center so they are the same size as the front piece.

3 With right sides together pin and machine stitch around front and back pieces along stitching line. Remove all tacking threads and Stitch and Tear stabilizer from the back of the embroidery.

4 Turn the pillow cover through the opening to the right side. Stitch the snaps in place on the back center seam and insert pillow form.

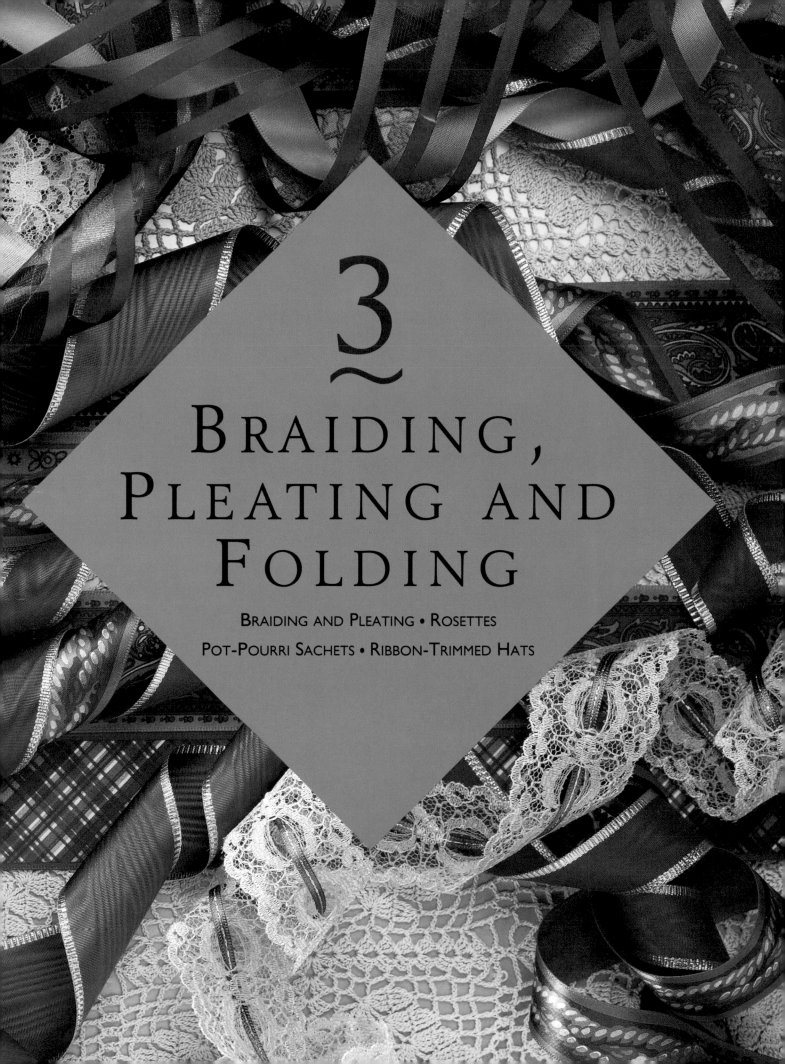

3

BRAIDING, PLEATING AND FOLDING

BRAIDING AND PLEATING • ROSETTES
POT-POURRI SACHETS • RIBBON-TRIMMED HATS

BRAIDING AND PLEATING

Conjure up a multitude of delightful rosettes and trimmings by pleating, folding, braiding, and weaving ribbons into three-dimensional forms.

SIMPLE BRAID

Braided ribbon can be used to trim all kinds of objects. It is especially useful for appliqué work along curved edges for which straight-edged ribbon is not suitable.

1 Pin three strands of narrow ribbon together on a board.

2 Braid in the usual way, keeping right side of the ribbon facing throughout.

3 When you have completed the required length, stitch or knot at each end to secure.

FOLDED BRAID

This method is particularly well suited to wide ribbon.

1 Pin three lengths of ribbon together on a board.

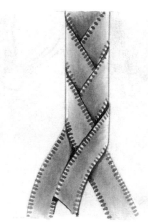

2 Braid, folding each outside strand towards the middle as you work. Stitch or knot at each end to secure when you have completed the required length.

FIVE-STRAND BRAID

This technique works best with narrow ribbon.

1 Pin five lengths of ribbon side-by-side on a board.

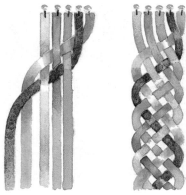

2 Working from one edge, bring the outside strand to the center, taking it under the adjacent strand, over the next and so on as shown.

3 Repeat until your braid is the required length. Stitch at each end to secure.

LOOP BRAID

This type of braid can be left loose for a three-dimensional effect or be pressed flat.

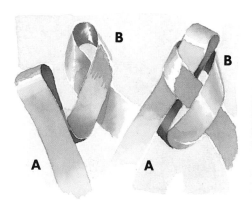

1 Form a loop in one end of a ribbon (A). Form another loop (B) and pass through first loop.

SIMPLE PLEAT

You can create a variety of effects from pleated ribbon for use in appliqué work or as a trim. To calculate the amount of ribbon you need, triple the length of your intended finished pleat.

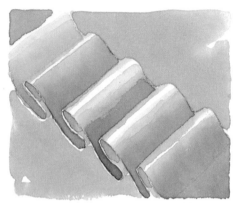

1 Fold and press the ribbon as shown.
2 Secure by topstitching either along one edge or down the center according to the effect desired.

BOX PLEAT

Box pleated wide ribbon provides an attractive home furnishing trim. Ribbon amounts are as for simple pleats.

1 Fold the ribbon as shown and press.

2 Take the long end of ribbon A, fold it to form a new loop and insert through the first loop.
3 Take the long end of ribbon B, fold to form a new loop and insert through the new loop in ribbon A.

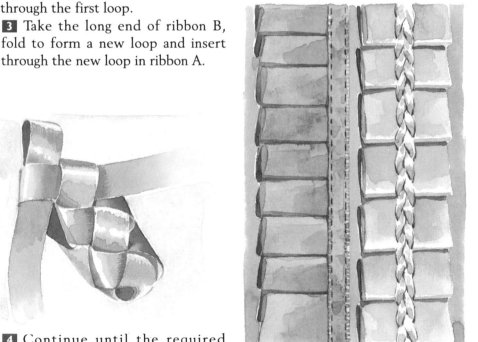

4 Continue until the required length is completed. Pin or stitch at each end to secure.

3 Conceal the stitching with a length of appliquéd ribbon or ribbon braid.

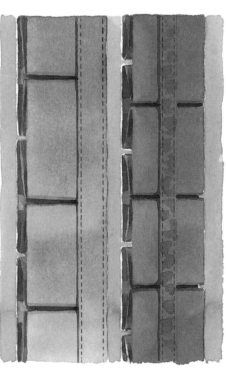

2 Secure by topstitching along one edge or along the center.
3 Conceal the topstitching as for simple pleats.

RIBBON BUTTON

This simple folded button provides a neat finish to rosettes and can also be used as a trim on its own.

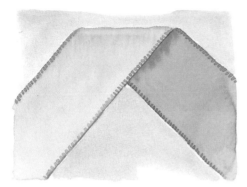

1 Fold a length of ribbon in half as shown.

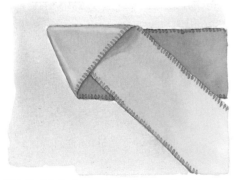

2 Fold left end under right (seen here on wrong side).

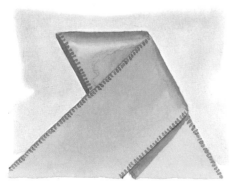

3 Turn to right side and continue to fold ribbon as shown.

4 Continue working in this way until button is completed.

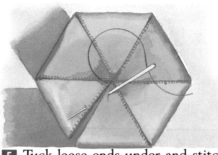

5 Tuck loose ends under and stitch to secure.

GATHERING

Ribbon can be gathered in various ways to produce a number of different effects. The techniques depend largely on the type of ribbon used.

WOVEN-EDGE – SIMPLE GATHERING

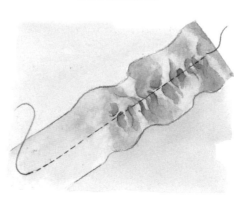

1 Gather the woven-edge ribbon by machine stitching a row of long loosely tensioned stitches along one edge or down the center of the ribbon.

2 Pull the lower thread from one end to gather, easing the ribbon along its length as you work.

WOVEN-EDGE – SHELL GATHERING

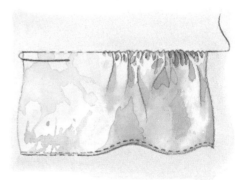

A variation on simple gathering, this effect is produced by hand-stitching a zig-zag line down the length of the ribbon and gathering as above.

WIRE-EDGE

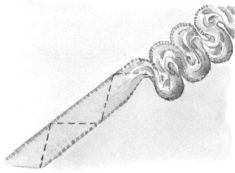

1 Gather wire-edge ribbon by freeing both ends of the wire from one edge of the ribbon. Secure one end by folding it over.
2 Pull the free end, easing the ribbon along its length to gather.
3 Trim excess wire and secure.

ROSETTES

Rosettes add a designer touch to home furnishings and clothing. Woven edge satin ribbon has been used on all the rosettes in this section.

RIBBON LILY

This 4½in (10.5cm) diameter rosette has 24 lily petals.

MATERIALS

- 2½yd (2.10m) of 1½in (39mm) wide ribbon

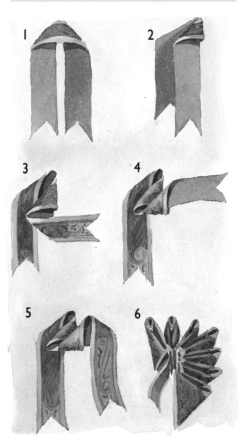

1 Form 24 petals as shown. After folding each petal, stitch at base to adjacent petal to hold in place.

2 When you have made 24 points, trim excess ribbon, overlap raw edges and stitch together, hiding seam inside last point.

3 Finish by concealing center with a covered button, beads or ribbon rose in matching or coordinating colors.

RIBBON DAISY

1 Make a ribbon lily as described.

2 Before finishing, turn in alternate points and stitch to secure at center.

FLAT RIBBON LILY

This can be made as an individual rosette sewn onto buckram or it may be sewn directly onto an item of clothing or home furnishing. For individual rosettes, in addition to the materials described for the ribbon lily above, you will need a circle of buckram or other fabric the diameter of the finished rosette.

1 Make a ribbon lily as described.

2 Pin each point to the buckram or fabric, ensuring they are facing in the same direction and are evenly distributed around its circumference. Stitch each point in place. Then stitch center and add chosen finish.

ADDING LOOPS

If you are making an individual rosette, you may wish to stitch loops of contrasting or coordinating ribbon between each petal point. You will need an extra 2¼yd (2m) of ⅝in (15mm) ribbon.

1 Cut twenty-four 3¼in (8cm) lengths of ribbon. Fold each length in half and press.

2 Insert each loop between petal points, stitching to secure at base, and point as shown.

FAN ROSETTE

This 7in (18cm) diameter semi-circular rosette is made from satin ribbon and uses four colors.

MATERIALS

- 1¼yd (1m) of 1½in (39mm) ribbon (color A – outer pleat)
- 1½yd (1.40m) of ⅞in (23mm) ribbon (color B – inner pleat)
- 1½yd (1.40m) of ⅞in (23mm) ribbon (color C – outer row of points)
- 1¼yd (1m) of ⅞in (23mm) ribbon (color D – inner row of points)
- 6¾in (17cm) diameter semi-circle of buckram.

1 Pleat color A ribbon (see Simple pleating, page 51) and stitch through all layers around circumference of buckram, approximately ¾in (2cm) in from edge.

2 Secure back fold of each pleat through center of width to buckram.

3 Pleat 28in (70cm) of color B ribbon and stitch at base to buckram through all layers so that top of pleat overlaps the first row by approximately ½in (1cm).

4 Cut twelve 3¾in (9cm) lengths of color C ribbon and eleven 3¾in (9cm) lengths of color D ribbon. Fold each point as shown. Stitch to secure and press.

5 Stitch five color C points (selvage side down) to buckram equally spaced under the second row of pleats so that the base of each point roughly aligns with the base of the pleat. Stitch a further four points of color C between each point of previous row at same height.

6 Stitch five color D points at equal intervals approximately ¼in (6mm) below previous row.

7 Stitch a further four color D points between each one of previous row at same height.

8 Stitch one color C point at center ½in (1cm) lower than previous row, followed by two further color C points on either side at same height.

9 To make center bow, cut 12in (30cm) of ribbon B and fold at center as shown. Cut two 8in (20cm) lengths of ribbon B, fold each in half, stitch to tail fold and stitch the resulting bow to center of rosette.

10 Take the two remaining points of ribbon D. Tuck raw ends of one point inside the other and stitch over center of bow.

FLORETTE ROSETTE

A rosette of this type can be made from woven-edge (as here) or wire-edged ribbon. It would make a truly charming hair or hat decoration.

MATERIALS

- 2⅛yd (1.90m) of ⅞in (23mm) gold edge ribbon
- 5¼in (13cm) diameter circle of buckram

1 Cut fourteen 5¼in (13cm) lengths of ribbon.

2 To make florettes, stitch raw ends of each ribbon length together and gather one selvage edge tightly.

3 Stitch nine florettes evenly around circle of buckram, about ½in (1cm) in from edge. Stitch four florettes to form an inner circle and the last florette in the center.

PETAL ROSETTE

This attractive spiral rosette can be finished with the center of your choice. It is shown here with a florette center and with a center medallion.

PETAL ROSETTE WITH FLORETTE

MATERIALS

- 3yd (2.70m) of ⅞in (23mm) ribbon (color A – petals)
- 10in (25cm) of ⅞in (23mm) wire-edge ribbon (color B – outer florette)
- 7½in (18cm) of ⅞in (23mm) wire-edge (color C – inner florette)

1 Cut twenty 5in (12cm) lengths of color A ribbon.

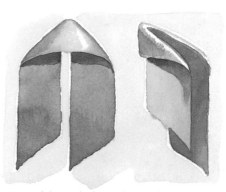

2 Fold each length to form petals as shown and secure with a stitch or with fusible web (at base only).

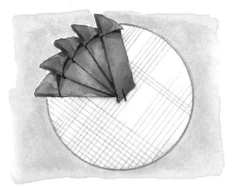

3 Pin each petal to the buckram to form a spiral as shown. Stitch through buckram at center and edge to secure.

4 Tightly gather one edge (see page 52) of ribbon B to create circle. Stitch raw ends together and stitch to center of rosette.

5 Repeat above using ribbon C.

6 Make a stitched rose (see page 97) and stitch to center of florette.

PETAL ROSETTE WITH CENTER MEDALLION

A rosette of this design was used to trim the ends of the Neck Roll Pillow on page 22.

MATERIALS

- 66in (1.7m) of ⅞in (23mm) ribbon
- 39in (1m) of ⅛in (3mm) ribbon
- 2¾in (7cm) diameter circle of matching fabric or wide ribbon
- 2½in (6cm) diameter circle of buckram

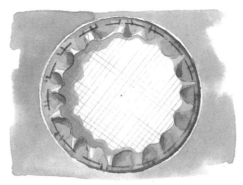

1 Cover buckram with fabric to make center medallion. Turn to wrong side and stitch close to edge. Trim excess fabric.

2 Make 14 petal points (see page 55) from the ⅞in ribbon

3 Place in a spiral on the wrong side of the medallion as shown. Stitch or glue to secure at center.

4 Cut the ⅛in ribbon into three equal lengths and make a flat braid (see page 50). Press and stitch around edge of medallion, folding raw edges of braid to wrong side. Stitch to secure and trim excess.

CATHERINE WHEEL ROSETTE

This simple 3½in (8cm) diameter rosette can be made with or without tails.

MATERIALS

- 1¼yd (1m) of ⅞in (23mm) ribbon
- 1½in (4cm) diameter circle of buckram
- A button covered with fabric or ribbon

1 Cut fourteen 2in (5cm) lengths of ribbon. Fold these in half and press.

2 Catch corners together and pin ribbon pieces on buckram as shown. Stitch to buckram at center to secure. Stitch button to center.

3 Stitch equal lengths of spare ribbon to back of buckram to form tail if required.

POT-POURRI SACHETS

These pot-pourri sachets decorated with braided, pleated, and woven ribbon are a delightful way of bringing garden scents into the home.

ROUND SACHET

MATERIALS

Ribbons (all singleface satin)
- 4½yd (4m) of ⅛in (3mm) wide in light color
- 4½yd (4m) of ⅛in (3mm) wide in dark color

Other materials
- One circle matching fabric 6in (15cm) diameter
- Two 6in (15cm) semi-circles of fabric plus ½in (1cm) seam allowance along straight edges
- Approximately 5½in (14cm) length of narrow Velcro
- 4¾in (12cm) square of iron-on interfacing
- Sewing thread

1 Cut twenty 5in (12cm) lengths of both the dark and light ribbon and prepare a zig-zag weave (see page 18) 4in (10cm) square.

2 Cut a 4in (10cm) diameter circle from the weave and machine stitch with a zig-zag to center of fabric .

3 Cut remaining light ribbon into three equal lengths and braid together. Do the same with the dark ribbon.

4 Cover raw edges of weaving with the light braid, and stitch in place.

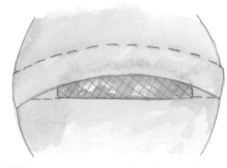

5 Turn in a single hem along straight edges of fabric semi-circles and machine stitch Velcro in place to close.

6 With right sides together machine stitch around edges. Turn through to right side, handstitch dark braid around edge and fill with pot pourri.

SQUARE SACHET

MATERIALS

Ribbons (all singleface satin)
- 16in (40cm) of ⅞in (23mm) dark green
- 2yd (1.80m) of ⅛in (3mm) dark green
- 12in (30cm) of ¼in (7mm) dark green

Other materials
- One piece fabric 7in (17cm) square
- Two pieces fabric 7in by 3¾in (17cm by 9.5cm)
- Short length of narrow Velcro

1 Fold one square of fabric across the diagonal and press to form guide-line. Open out.

2 Make small pleats in ⅞in (23mm) ribbon until it is the same length as the diagonal line and machine stitch in place along the center.

3 Cut ⅛in (3mm) ribbon into three equal lengths and braid together.

4 Stitch three rows of braid: one in center of pleated ribbon to cover stitching, and one across each corner, 2in (5cm) away from the central braid.

5 Make two small bows from ¼in (7mm) ribbon and stitch onto braiding.

6 Turn in ½in (1cm) hems on two long edges of the back pieces, stitch in Velcro, and finish as for round sachet, omitting braid trim.

RIBBON-TRIMMED HATS

*Embellish a plain felt, straw, or velvet hat with ribbon
roses and rosettes to create your own unique look.*

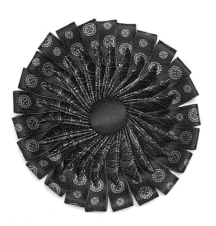

FELT HAT WITH
LILY ROSETTE

The lily rosette with a coordinating
outer circle of ribbon loops and a
central cover button makes a dramatic hat trim (see page 53 for instructions for making the rosette). A band
of ribbon in coordinating colors com-
pletes the trim.

WEDDING HAT

A very soft feminine look can be
achieved with a dainty band of sheer
ribbon entwined around a ribbon or
cord hat band. This straw hat is perfect for a summer wedding or garden
party.

FELT HAT WITH
CATHERINE WHEEL
ROSETTE

This delicate rosette and matching
hat band in a rich printed satin ribbon
discreetly complement the rich red
of the hat. See page 56 for instructions for making the rosette.

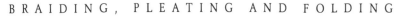

1 Cut ribbon into 3½in (8.5cm) lengths as follows: 10 color A; 9 color B; 6 color C.

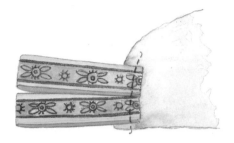

2 Fold ribbon A lengths in half and stitch equally spaced around curved edge of buckram as shown.

VELVET HAT WITH SEMI-CIRCULAR ROSETTE

A thirties-style cockade finished with a central rose looks perfect on a cloche or similar period hat. A tail of ribbon at the top or bottom can add a touch of whimsy. Instructions for making the rosette are given right.

SEMI-CIRCULAR ROSETTE

This 6in (15cm) diameter rosette makes an original finish and can be seen on the hat above.

3 Form each length of ribbon B into petal points as shown and stitch to buckram under previous row. Each petal point should slightly overlap its neighbor.

4 Complete third row using six ribbon C points as second row.

5 Finish with a stitched rose in the remaining ribbon B (see page 97). Tails can be added if desired.

> ### MATERIALS
>
> - 1½yd (1.40m) of ⅝in (15mm) ribbon (color A – first row)
> - 1¼yd (1.10m) of ⅝in (15mm) ribbon (color B – second row)
> - 24in (60cm) of ⅝in (15mm) ribbon (color C – third row)
> - 4½in (11cm) diameter semi-circular piece of buckram

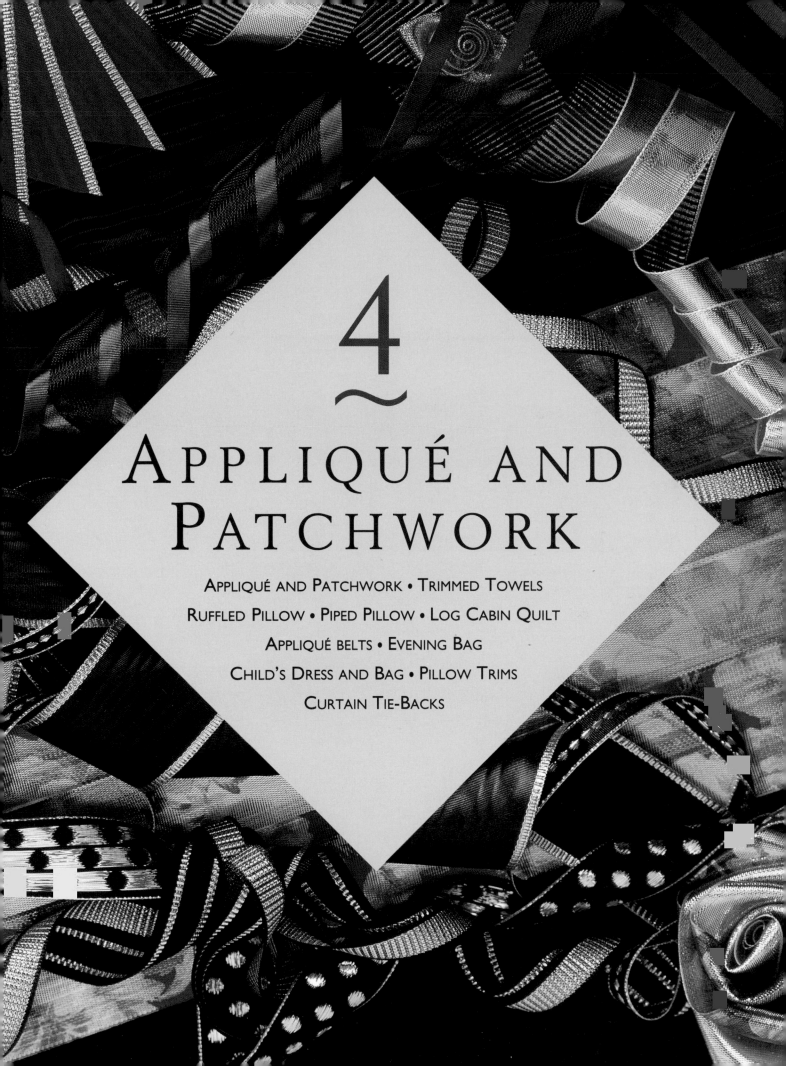

4
~
APPLIQUÉ AND
PATCHWORK

Appliqué and Patchwork • Trimmed Towels
Ruffled Pillow • Piped Pillow • Log Cabin Quilt
Appliqué belts • Evening Bag
Child's Dress and Bag • Pillow Trims
Curtain Tie-Backs

APPLIQUÉ AND PATCHWORK

Woven-edge ribbons are simple to use for appliqué and patchwork. Because there are no raw edges they can easily be applied either by hand or machine sewing.

HELPFUL HINTS

- When machine stitching, always work in the same direction on both edges to prevent puckering.
- Before you trim a garment with ribbon make sure it is color fast and shrink resistant.
- Plan the design on paper to calculate quantities and widths. Remember to allow for seams and neatening ends.
- Ribbon is best applied to flat pieces of fabric before the garment is made up, but if trimming a ready made article, open up the seams a little to allow ribbon joins to be hidden inside the garment.
- Mark the design lines with dressmaker's chalk. Lay ribbon along the lines and position with a fabric glue stick or tacking stitches.
- When machine stitching velvet, use a zipper foot to avoid crushing the pile.
- Use polyester thread, and if the ribbon puckers, try a larger stitch or loosen the top tension.
- If you prefer to handsew, use a tiny hem stitch.
- If you have a twin needle attachment adjust it to be slightly narrower than your ribbon so that you can stitch down both edges at the same time.
- If you have a large number of ribbons to sew next to one another, fix them onto lightweight iron-on interfacing before sewing.

IDEAS FOR RIBBON PATCHWORK

You can bring new dimensions to the time-honored craft of patchwork using ribbon appliqué designs inspired by traditional patchwork quilts. Try any of the following designs, scaling the squares up or down by increasing or decreasing the rows of ribbons.

MISSOURI PUZZLE

This patchwork appliqué is worked directly onto fabric and the ribbon is woven at the intersections. The illustration shows 12 lengths of ribbon divided as follows (the widths of colors A, B, and C do not need to be the same): six green, four orange, and two yellow. Following the diagram, position and attach ribbons using fabric glue stick paying particular attention to woven intersections before stitching.

STRING QUILTED DIAMOND

Made from four small blocks joined to form a diamond effect on a large square. Each small square is worked on interfacing with ribbons stitched diagonally.

LOG CABIN PATCHWORK

In this type of patchwork light and dark ribbons are used to frame the small center square.

COURTHOUSE STEPS

This is a log cabin variation constructed by stitching pairs of ribbons around the center square. The pairs always match but a variety of light and dark shades of plain or printed ribbon can be alternated as the square is built up.

PINEAPPLE

The center square of the pineapple is made from four horizontal ribbons. The next row consists of four ribbons placed diagonally across the corners. Raw edges are concealed by ribbons placed around the center square. Continue the sequence with another set of diagonals and so on. The diagonals can be in a variety of shades and the straight ribbon in one color or coordinated colors ranging from light to dark.

MITERED CORNERS

Mitering is a neat way of creating a right-angled corner with appliquéd ribbon.

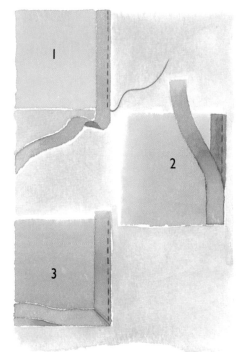

1 Stitch ribbon to corner.
2 Lay ribbon end back along stitched edge.
3 Fold ribbon down to lie horizontally, making a diagonal fold at the corner; press lightly.

4 Stitch across diagonal fold line.
5 Continue stitching ribbon edge.

APPLYING RIBBON EDGINGS

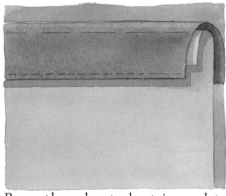

Press the edge to be trimmed to right side of fabric. Tack the ribbon on the fold, covering the raw edge, then topstitch (wrongside first) along both edges of ribbon.

RIBBON CASINGS

Ribbon—at least ⅝in (15mm) wide—makes an attractive casing for drawstrings or elastic in clothing or furnishing projects.

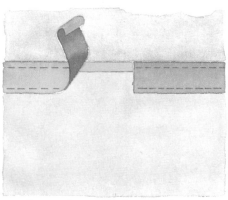

1 Press the top edge of the casing to the right side along seam line.
2 Trim to ¼in (6mm), and topstitch ribbon to right side of fabric, covering raw edge.
3 Fold in ribbon edges for the case opening. Run narrow ribbon through casing on a safety pin, and cut ends diagonally to prevent fraying.

TRIMMED TOWELS

Give plain towels a designer finish by applying a grosgrain ribbon trim, adding Battenberg or Cluny lace for a special touch.

MATERIALS

- Ribbon to fit towel width plus turnings
- Light weight iron-on interfacing
- Sewing thread
- Fabric glue stick

APPLYING THE RIBBON

1 Fuse light weight iron-on interfacing to the wrong side of the ribbon, cutting the interfacing a fraction smaller than the width of the ribbon.

2 Position the ribbon on the towel and pin to secure. Turn the ends under and fix with fabric glue stick.

3 Machine stitch the ribbon on with a small zig-zag, working in the same direction on both edges, and stitch twice across the ends.

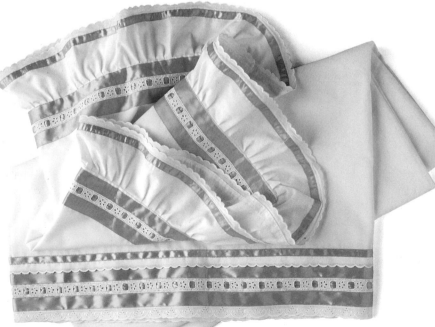

Basic bed and table linen can be luxuriously transformed with appliquéd ribbon. Choose plain or printed satins or jacquards to complement your existing color scheme. And perhaps add a touch of lace or broderie anglaise.

RUFFLED PILLOW

*This pillow, with its appliquéd ribbons in deep, rich colors
on a contrasting fabric, makes a bold statement.*

THE PILLOW PIECES

1 For the pillow front cut one 15in (38cm) square from the fabric. For the pillow back to include a zipper, cut one piece 15in by 12½in (38cm by 32cm), and one piece 15in by 4in (38cm by 10cm).

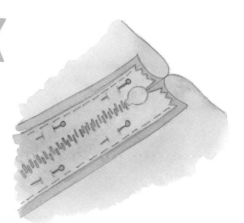

2 With right sides together and using tacking stitches, join the back pieces with a ¾in (2cm) tacked seam. Machine stitch end sections outside zipper length. Press seam open and pin, tack and then machine stitch zipper in final position.

WORKING THE APPLIQUÉ

1 On the pillow front, mark the center point on each edge with a pin.

2 Fold each corner diagonally from pin to pin and press, then open fabric out again. The pressed creases will form guidelines for the ribbon.

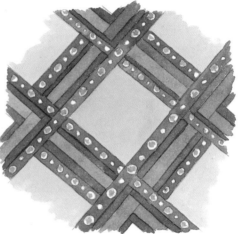

3 Machine stitch patterned ribbon along guidelines to form a diamond shape, then continue stitching ribbon in groups of five in the following order: patterned, plain ⅜in (9mm), plain ⅞in (23mm), plain ⅜in (9mm), patterned.

MAKING UP

1 From the remaining fabric, cut strips 4in (10cm) wide for the ruffle. With right sides together, join to make a 95½in (240cm) length.

2 Join ends to make a loop, then fold in half lengthwise wrong sides together. Gather along raw edges through both thicknesses, and adjust to fit pillow front. With right sides together, pin and tack ruffle to front.

3 Open zipper and then join back and front by pinning and then machine stitching pieces with right sides together along seam line.

PIPED PILLOW

For a soft, rich effect, woven-edge ribbons in coordinating colors have been used for this pillow cover.

MATERIALS

Ribbons
- 5yd (4.50m) of ⅞in (23mm) wide patterned
- 2½yd (2.30m) of ⅞in (23mm) wide plain
- 5yd (4.50m) of ¼in (7mm) wide plait

- 1¼yd (1m) of 48in (122cm) wide cotton chintz
- 2½yd (2.20m) piping
- 18in (45cm) zipper

Other materials
- One pillow form 22in (55cm) square

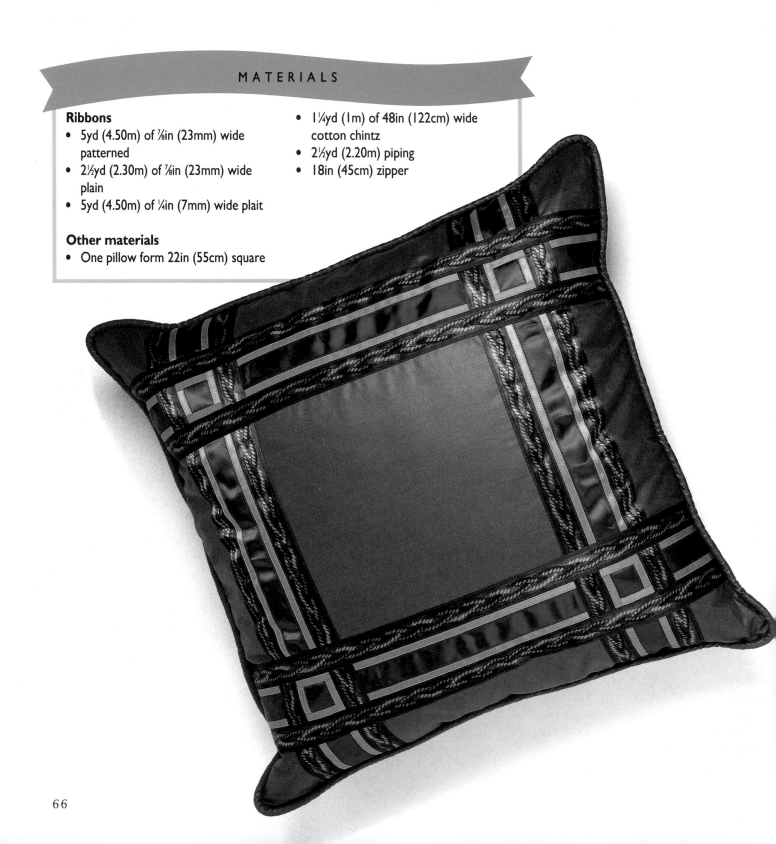

66

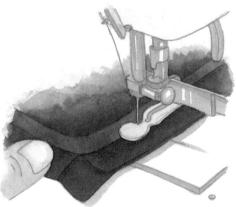

THE PILLOW PIECES

1 From fabric cut one 23in (58cm) square for the pillow front. For the back, cut one piece 23in by 19¾in (58cm by 50cm); and one piece 23in by 4¾in (58cm by 12cm).

2 To make the pillow back, follow the instructions on page 65.

WORKING THE APPLIQUÉ

1 On the front square, mark 4in (10cm) in from each side horizontally and vertically with a pin.

2 Fold and lightly press across the marks to form guidelines for ribbons and sew them on with machine stitching in order as shown on the diagram.

1 From remaining fabric, cut 1¼in (3cm) bias strips and join as shown to make a 88in (220cm) length.

2 Cover piping with bias strips and tack around edge of pillow front.

3 Machine piping to right side of cushion front along seam line.

4 With right sides facing, pin and machine stitch front and back pieces together, using a zipper foot if you have one. Turn through to right side and press.

LOG CABIN QUILT

In this log cabin quilt, plain satin ribbons in contrasting colors give a strong three-dimensional effect. For a larger quilt, simply increase the number of squares.

WORKING THE PATCHWORK

1 From interfacing cut 24 squares each 10in (25cm).

2 Draw diagonals from corner to corner on each square, using pencil and ruler.

3 Cutting ribbon to length as necessary, start by sewing on the central shocking pink ribbon square. Following diagrams, machine stitch on ribbons, each time covering the edges of the previous ribbon.

4 Each square is worked in the same way. Complete the required number.

1

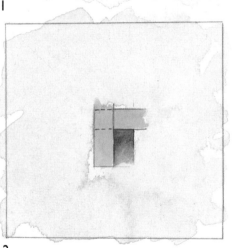

2

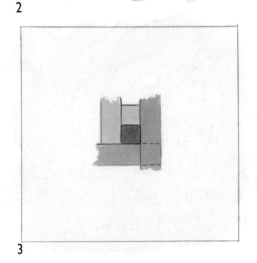

3

4

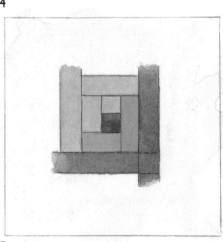

5

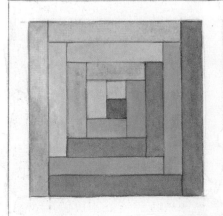

6

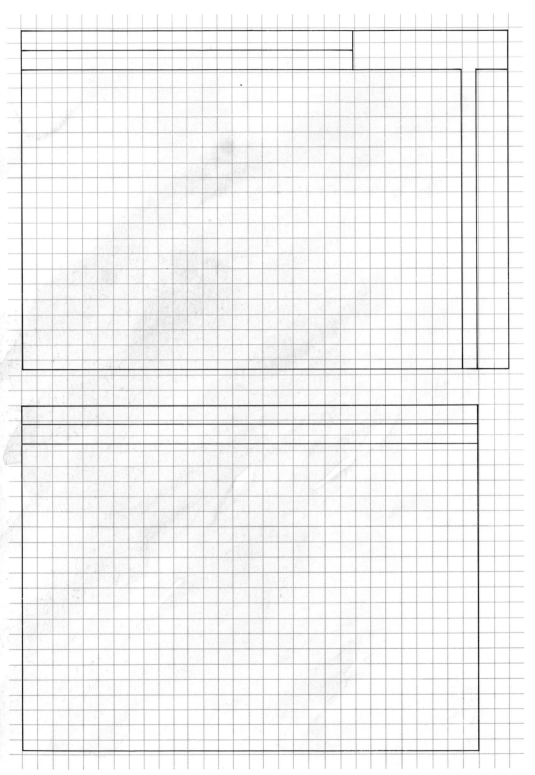

JOINING THE SQUARES

1 Cut a piece of fabric 40in by 60in (100cm by 150cm) and tack all the patchwork squares in place.

2 Using the appropriate colored ribbon (pink or purple) machine stitch continuous strips to cover the edges of the squares and to form one large patchwork (the quilt top).

MAKING THE QUILT

1 From remaining fabric cut one piece 40in by 57in (100cm by 145cm) and one piece 3½in by 40in (9cm by 100cm).

2 Turn in ⅜in (1cm) along one short edge of each piece. Overlap edges by ⅜in (1cm) and position Velcro or snaps to make case opening. If using snaps, make a narrow double seam. Velcro can be sewn over the raw edges.

3 With wrong sides together, tack front and back pieces together.

4 Cut two pieces of fabric 2¼in by 60in (6cm by 150cm) and use to bind sides of quilt.

5 Cut two pieces of fabric 2¼in by 43¼in (6cm by 110cm) and bind top and bottom edges.

Scale 1 square = 2in (5cm)

APPLIQUÉ BELTS

Use appliqué techniques to create your own belts from ribbon in the colors, textures, and prints that complement your wardrobe.

Simply cover a piece of substantial interfacing with bands of ribbon. First cut the interfacing to the desired finished size and shape. The length of a belt is the size of your waist plus turnings.

Use a fabric marker to work out positions for the ribbon and calculate the quantities accordingly. You can add further surface texture by incorporating embroidery stitches or applying narrow ribbon over wider bands using a straight or zig-zag stitch. Always take special care with the first ribbon as this will be your guide line for stitching all subsequent ribbons. Finish the edge of the belt with a ribbon braid or make a binding in the same fabric as your garment fabric.

Create your own belt designs to provide the perfect finishing touch to any outfit. Horizontal bands, diagonal stripes, coordinating colors or contrasting textures – the possibilities are endless.

Ribbon appliqué gives the opportunity for creating matching accessories. Here two black evening bags and a belt with appliquéd metallic ribbons would provide a sophisticated accent to a simple black outfit.

EVENING BAG

The magnificent ranges of Lurex and embroidered ribbons are perfect for decorating party accessories. This subtle Lurex print gives a plain bag a glamorous image.

THE BAG PIECES

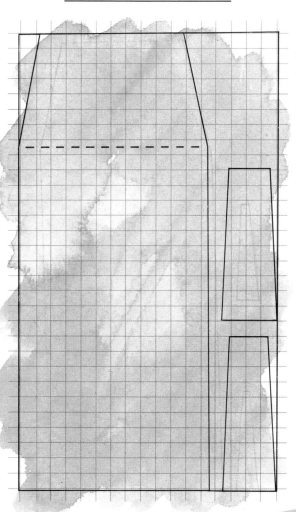

Scale 1 square = 1¾in (2cm)

1 Make a paper pattern, following diagram, and cut out bag shape once in all fabrics. Tack taffeta piece to interfacing.

2 Machine stitch the piece of metallic ribbon along the center line, then machine stitch lengths of ⅜in (9mm) grosgrain either side.

MATERIALS

Ribbons
- 24in (60cm) of 1½in (39mm) wide metallic floral
- 1⅓yd (1.20m) of ⅜in (9mm) wide gold grosgrain
- 11yd (10m) of ¹⁄₁₆in (1.5mm) wide gold grosgrain

Other materials
- One piece black taffeta 10¾in by 32¼in (27cm by 82cm)
- One piece heavy weight interfacing 10¾in by 32¼in (27cm by 82cm)
- One piece lining 10¾in by 32¼in (27cm by 82cm)
- Snap

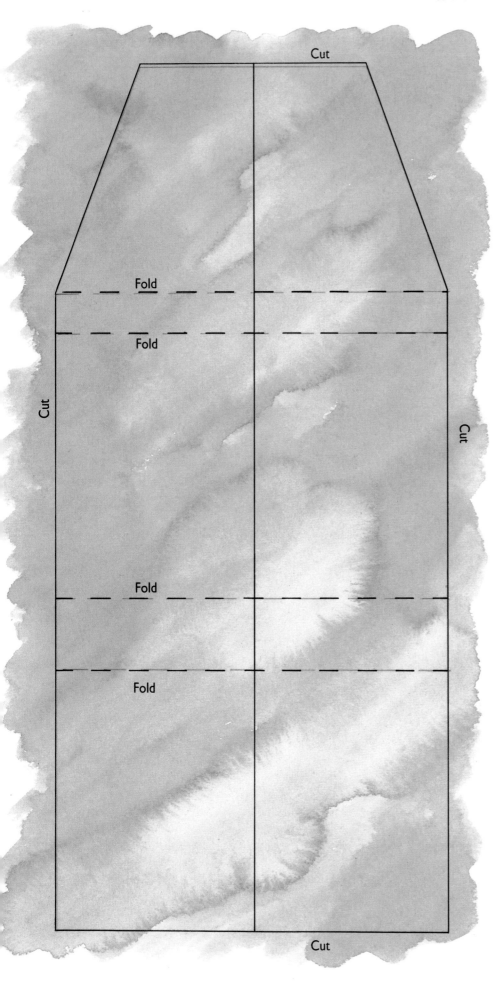

Cut

Fold

Fold

Cut

Cut

Fold

Fold

Cut

MAKING-UP THE BAG

1 Cut two side panels from taffeta and lining. On taffeta pieces, make darts, then sew to main piece to form a bag shape with flap.

2 Turn in all raw edges and hand-stitch in place.

3 Cut the 1/16in (1.5mm) grosgrain into three equal lengths. Braid together (see Simple braid, page 50) and handsew around flap edges and across top.

4 Cut remaining braiding into two equal lengths and attach to either side of top to form shoulder strap.

5 Make up lining as main piece and handstitch into place.

6 To finish, sew snaps in place to fasten.

CHILD'S DRESS AND BAG

To make this pretty child's dress, look for a commercial paper pattern with a yoked design.

MATERIALS

Ribbons for dress – amounts according to measurements of hem, yoke and cuffs
- 1½in (39mm) printed
- ³⁄₁₆in (5mm) plain
- ⅝in (15mm) printed
- ⅛in (3mm) plain

Ribbons for shoulder bag
- 3yd (2.85m) of ⅞in (23mm) printed
- 3ft (90cm) of ³⁄₁₆in (5mm) plain
- 3½yd (3.30m) of ⅛in (3mm) plain

Other materials
- 17¾in by 7in (45cm by 18cm) heavy weight interfacing
- 17¾in by 7in (45cm by 18cm) lining
- One snap
- Choice of pattern
- Materials as pattern
- Three ready-made roses

THE DRESS

1 Cut out pieces, following pattern instructions. Make up lower frill, shoulder frill, yoke front and back, and cuffs, but do not seam to rest of dress at this point.

2 Add ribbon to these pieces as follows:

3 To lower frill – one band each of 1½in (39mm) printed, ³⁄₁₆in (5mm) plain, ⅝in (15mm) printed.

4 To shoulder frill – one band each ⅝in (15mm) printed, ³⁄₁₆in (5mm) plain.

5 Centrally on yoke front and 2in (5cm) away each side – one band ³⁄₁₆in (5mm) plain, two bands ⅝in (15mm) printed.

6 Sew back yoke to match, omitting center band.

7 On cuff – one band ⅝in (15mm) printed.

8 Make up dress as pattern instructions, and sew roses onto yoke.

9 Plait ⅛in (3mm) ribbon (see Simple braid, page 50) and stitch round collar edge. Sew roses on to yoke.

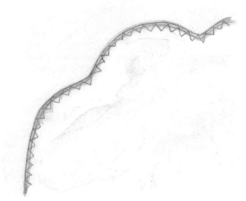

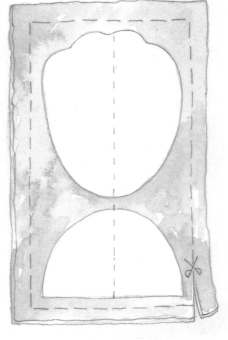

THE SHOULDER BAG

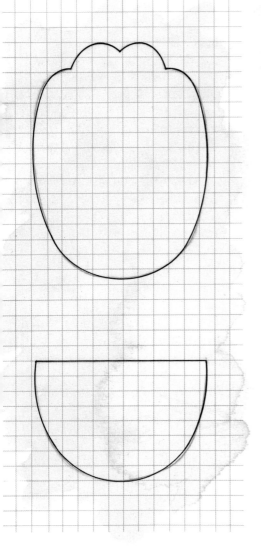

6 Turn to right side. Zig-zag stitch around raw edges of bag flap.

1 Make a paper pattern of the two bag pieces from the diagram, lay it on the interfacing and cut out a rectangle as shown.

2 Starting from one long side, sew ribbons vertically down the length of the interfacing in the following order: two rows wide printed, one row narrow plain. Continue in the same order.

3 Lay the pattern pieces on the ribbon-decorated interfacing and cut out the pieces. Cut the same pieces in lining. With wrong sides together, tack to interfacing.

4 Cut a 6¼in (16cm) piece of wide printed ribbon, fold it in half lengthways and sew over the raw edge at the top of the front pocket piece.

5 With right sides together, join front and back pieces with a narrow seam and finish with zig-zag stitching.

7 Braid ⅛in (3mm) plain ribbon and handstitch around petal edges. Use remainder to make shoulder strap, and sew to inside of front flap.
8 Sew on a snap and ribbon roses.

Scale 1 square = ⅝in (15mm)

PILLOW TRIMS

These removable trims show a combination of appliqué and weaving, a novel way to embellish ready-made pillows. They are fastened at the back with Velcro.

5 Cut 1½in (39mm) ribbon into four pieces, fold each one in half and enclose loose ribbon ends. Tack, then stitch to secure.

MATERIALS

Ribbons – all ¼in (7mm) wide except where indicated.
Pink pillow
- 18¼yd (16.80m) black A
- 20¼yd (18.50m) turquoise B
- 1½yd (1.30m) of 1½in (39mm) wide black

Purple pillow
- 19¼yd (17.70m) yellow A
- 19¼yd (17.70m) orange B
- 1½yd (1.30m) of 1½in (39mm) yellow

Turquoise pillow
- 13yd (11.80m) pink A
- 18¼yd (16.80m) mauve B
- 7½yd (6.75m) pale turquoise C
- 1½yd (1.30m) of 1½in (39mm) mauve

Blue pillow
- 7½yd (6.75m) pink A
- 7½yd (6.75m) sea green B
- 3¾yd (3.40m) yellow C
- 1½yd (1.30m) 1½in (39mm) wide sea green

Other materials (for each pillow)
- One 15¾in (40cm) square pillow form
- 6¾in (17cm) square of craft-weight interfacing
- 6¾in (17cm) square of iron-on interfacing for weaving
- 4¾in (12cm) length Velcro

PINK PILLOW

1 Cut ribbon A and B into 33in (84cm) lengths.

2 Draw a 6in (15cm) square onto iron-on interfacing and zig-zag weave a square (see page 18), leaving 13½in (34.5cm) lengths of ribbon loose on all sides.

3 Place woven square in center of heavy interfacing and machine stitch around edge of weaving.

4 Carefully trim away excess interfacing close to machine stitches.

6 Cut Velcro in half and stitch to opposite ends of ribbon to fasten on underside of pillow.

TURQUOISE PILLOW

1 Cut ribbons A, B, and C into 33in (84cm) lengths.

2 Draw a 6in (15cm) square onto heavy interfacing and draw diagonals to find center.

PURPLE PILLOW

1 Cut ribbons A and B into 33in (84cm) lengths.

2 Weave five warp B and five weft A at the center of the heavy interfacing leaving 13½in (34.5cm) lengths loose as before.

BLUE PILLOW

1 Cut ribbons A, B and C into 33in (84cm) lengths.

2 Draw square as turquoise pillow. Working from outer edge inwards machine stitch five rows of ribbon in the following order A, B, C, B, A.

3 Sew four B and then four A on each side of center square in the order shown.

4 Continue from Step 4 of instructions for pink pillow.

3 Working from the center out around the square, machine stitch ribbons in the following order: one center square of A, one of B each side of pink, two of C, four of B, three of A. Leave 13½in (34.5cm) lengths loose on all sides.

4 Continue from Step 4 of instructions for pink pillow.

3 Carefully trim interfacing from center as well as outer edges.

4 Continue from Step 5 of instructions for pink pillow.

CURTAIN TIE-BACKS

*Evocative of hazy summer days, ribbons and roses give a
delightful feminine finish to piped tie-backs. Use ribbon
that matches your drapes to provide a subtle accent.*

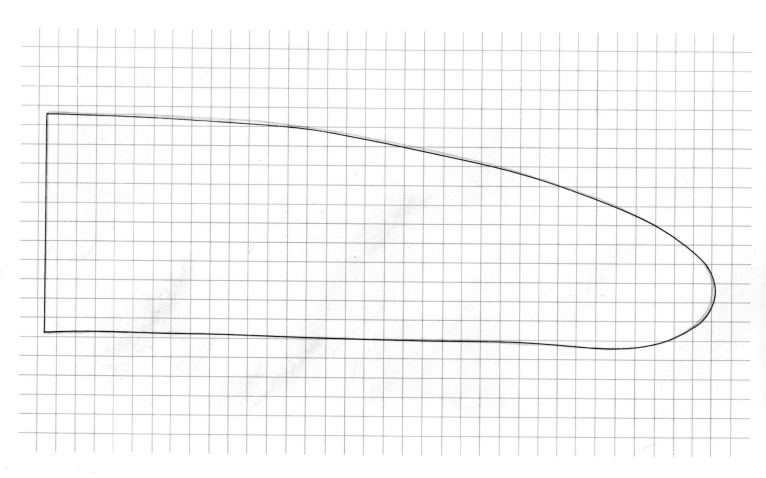

Scale I square = ½in (1cm)

MATERIALS

All quantities are for a pair.
- 2¾yd (2.50m) of ⅛in (3mm) doublefaced satin ribbon
- 44 ribbon rosebuds
- 16in by 32in (40cm by 80cm) of fabric
- 16in by 32in (40cm by 80cm) of pelmet quality interfacing
- 16in by 32in (40cm by 80cm) of paper-backed fusible web

- 16in by 32in (40cm by 80cm) of lining
- 3¼yd (3m) No 3 piping
- Four by ¾in (2cm) rings
- Thread
- Fabric marking pen or pencil; ruler

The instructions are for two tie-backs for a pair of drapes.

MAKING THE TIE-BACKS

1 Enlarge the grid diagram to make a paper pattern and cut out two pieces in fabric, two in interfacing and two in lining.

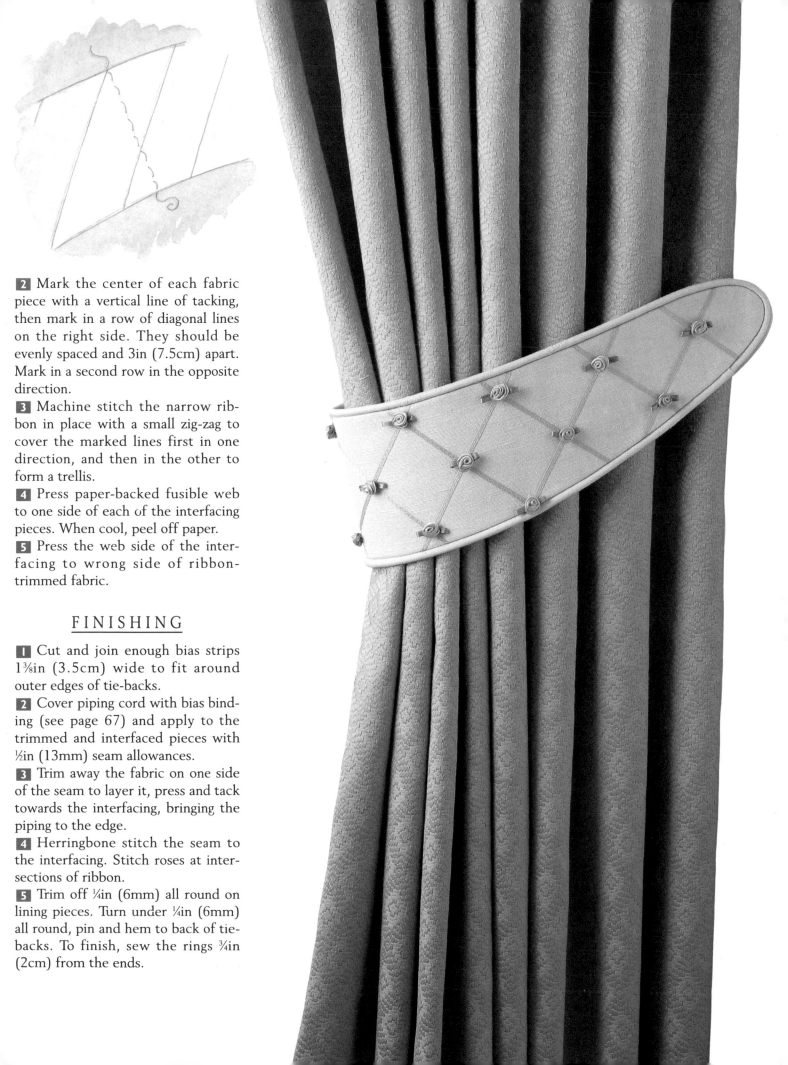

2 Mark the center of each fabric piece with a vertical line of tacking, then mark in a row of diagonal lines on the right side. They should be evenly spaced and 3in (7.5cm) apart. Mark in a second row in the opposite direction.

3 Machine stitch the narrow ribbon in place with a small zig-zag to cover the marked lines first in one direction, and then in the other to form a trellis.

4 Press paper-backed fusible web to one side of each of the interfacing pieces. When cool, peel off paper.

5 Press the web side of the interfacing to wrong side of ribbon-trimmed fabric.

FINISHING

1 Cut and join enough bias strips 1⅜in (3.5cm) wide to fit around outer edges of tie-backs.

2 Cover piping cord with bias binding (see page 67) and apply to the trimmed and interfaced pieces with ½in (13mm) seam allowances.

3 Trim away the fabric on one side of the seam to layer it, press and tack towards the interfacing, bringing the piping to the edge.

4 Herringbone stitch the seam to the interfacing. Stitch roses at intersections of ribbon.

5 Trim off ¼in (6mm) all round on lining pieces. Turn under ¼in (6mm) all round, pin and hem to back of tie-backs. To finish, sew the rings ¾in (2cm) from the ends.

5

BOW-MAKING

BOW-MAKING TECHNIQUES • PICTURE BOW

GIFT WRAPS • CHRISTMAS TREE BOWS • CHRISTMAS BASKET

EASTER BASKET

BOW-MAKING TECHNIQUES

*Bows are quick to make, using any type of ribbon.
Multiloop and layered bows suit more formal projects,
while hand-tied bows look pretty in informal arrangements.*

USING A NAIL BLOCK

You can speed up the bow making process and produce consistent-sized hand-tied bows with a simple homemade nail block. Simply drive two nails through a wooden block (almost any grade is suitable). The length of the nails and the distance between them determines the size of the finished bow, but they can be anything from 4in (100mm) to 10in (250mm) long. Simply loop the ribbon once or twice around the nails, pull tight and secure by tying the tails at the center.

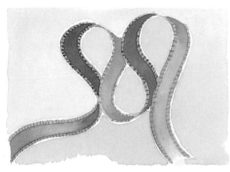

1 Arrange ribbon into two loops, holding one in each hand.

3 Fold left loop over right and under, tying into a bow.

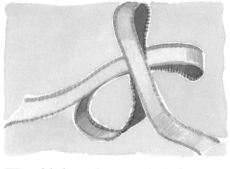

2 Fold the right over the left.

Brightly colored craft ribbon bows create an eye-catching finish to this cellophane-wrapped gift basket.

CLASSIC HAND-TIED BOW

Use these traditional bows for decorating craft projects, gift wrappings or as a clothing trim.

BASIC LOOP BOW

CENTER-BOUND BOW

DOUBLE BOW

These simple bows can be used on their own or combined to make other types such as layered bows.

1 Cut ribbon to twice the width of the finished bow plus a 2in (5cm) seam allowance and a little extra to allow for gathering the bow at the center. Overlap the raw ends to form a loop, and stitch to secure.

1 Cut a length of ribbon three times the desired width of the bow, plus a little extra to allow for gathering. Cut the edges diagonally to prevent fraying.

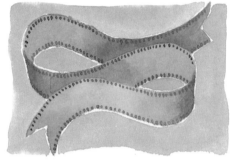

2 Loop the ribbon loosely around as shown above.

These showy bows look complicated, but in fact are very easy to make. They are made in exactly the same way as the basic loop bow.

1 Make two loops, one larger than the other. The ribbon for the second bow can be the same width as the first or narrower.

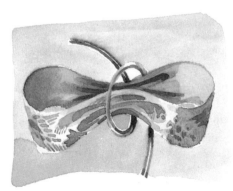

2 With the stitched edge at center back, flatten the loop slightly, pinch it together in the middle and either stitch down securely or bind florist's wire around the center. The wire method is better for stiff ribbon.

3 Use florist's wire or a narrow ribbon of a matching or contrasting texture or color to bind the center. Ease the ribbon end at the front to the back of the bow. You can finish off with a hand-tied bow or bind the ribbon around several times and secure at the back.

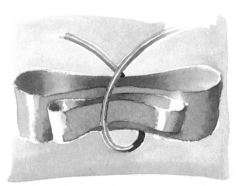

2 Lay the small loop on the large one and bind with florist's wire, then wrap a short piece of ribbon around the wire, and either sew or knot at the back.

LOOPED BOWS ON CARDBOARD

These looped bows are deceptively easy to make, and are ideal for decorating gifts or as hair accessories.

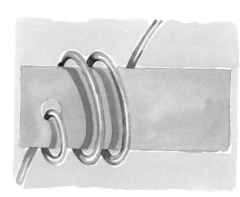

1 Cut a piece of card 1½in by 3in (4cm by 8cm) and make a small hole on left-hand side ½in (1cm) in from the edge. Thread a length of florist's wire through the hole and around the cardboard twice to secure.

2 Working from left to right on top of the cardboard make ribbon loops, securing each one with a turn of the wire. Leave a 4in (10cm) ribbon tail at each end.

3 Secure wire on underside of cardboard by twisting it around itself, cutting off the end.

3 A tail can be added if desired, by sewing or gluing on two additional pieces of ribbon at the back. Fix them at a slight angle, as shown.

LAYERED BOW

This bow takes the double bow one stage further by using several different-sized loops joined together. The ribbon for each layer should be the same width, and you can either make them all in the same color or vary them.

1 To make the base, or back of the bow, cut ribbon to desired length plus 1in (2.5cm) seam allowance. Overlap ends to form a loop, stitch, and flatten out loop.

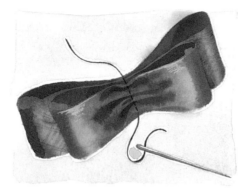

2 The next length of ribbon is cut shorter than the first. The exact measurement depends on the effect you want to create. Make the loop in the same way, and place it centrally on top of the first one. Stitch through both layers at center back, and pull stitches gently to gather the bow slightly.

3 Continue in the same way, making each layer shorter, until you have as many as you want. Finally, wrap a short length of ribbon around the center and stitch at back.

POMPON BOWS

A pompon bow is made from many loops of ribbon which are anchored tightly at the center with florist's wire before being separated to form a fluffy bow. The average pompon bow requires 3½yd (3.20m) of ribbon.

1 Begin with a loop of ribbon about 6in (15cm) across (you can adjust the size for a larger or smaller bow).

2 Wrap the ribbon around 10 times.

3 Flatten the loops and cut off triangles at each end as shown.

4 Bring the ends together in the middle, matching the cut triangles.

5 Wrap center with wire, and pull out loops, twisting them as you turn.

A basket wrapped in netting and trimmed with a sheer multiloop bow provides a touch of luxury to a simple gift.

MULTILOOP AND FLORIST'S BOWS

Wreaths and flowers often need ribbons arranged among them, with pine cones and other display materials to add color and texture. Florist's loops and bows have a small base and full top. The method for making them is similar to that for pompon bows, but the loops are squeezed

upwards and secured with wire to keep them upright.

1 Take a length of ribbon, about 2yd (1.80m), and squeeze it between your fingers approximately 2in (5cm) from one end.

2 Hold ribbon in one hand and make a loop in it with the other; pinch ribbon and hold securely.

3 Add another loop to the other side of bow and pinch as before, twisting ribbon as necessary to keep right side of ribbon to the outside of the bow.

4 Continue making loops, alternating from side to side and pinching each one firmly in the center until at least four loops have been made on each side.

5 To secure, wrap wire around center of bow and twist firmly. Pull loops into shape.

6 To turn this into a florist's bow, simply make a small loop in the center with the last tail and wire to secure.

Impressive to look at but easy to make, our traditional florist style bow is suitable for almost every occasion. Use them for decorating a floral arrangement, tying up a wrapped package or gift basket or finishing off a wreath or garland, or decorating a room for a special occasion. The technique is versatile and any size or type of ribbon can be used. You can design your bow as you make it.

PICTURE BOW

Enhance a picture with a bow centered above the frame, or make a group arrangement in colors to match the frame or mount.

1 Placing the 1½in (39mm) ribbon centrally on the wider one, fuse the two pieces of ribbon to each other using fusible web.

2 Make two loops about 4in (10cm) wide, with a small overlap in the middle and bind in the middle with florist's wire.

3 Cover the wire with a piece of ribbon, securing it at the back with a couple of stitches.

4 Stitch bow tails of whatever length you require at the back of bow, and finish with a loop to attach to a picture hook.

GIFT WRAPS

Have fun choosing ribbon colors and prints to match the mood of the occasion. Soft and romantic, bright and amusing, or simply wild.

Multiloop bows (see page 86) are a popular choice for gift wraps. It is up to you to decide how many loops, the length of the tails and what style to have the center. To determine how much ribbon each bow will need first decide how long each loop will be and multiply that amount by two, then multiply this figure by the number of loops that you want. Add the total length of the desired tail ends to that figure and round up by about 6in (10cm) to get the total amount needed for creating your style bow.

A patterned ribbon has been used to bind the parcel (below) and a multiloop bow in yellow and red provides the finish.

A wide ribbon tied with a simple knot (left) is an easy but effective solution.

A multiloop bow in the same ribbon as the binding is a classic gift wrap.

Red and pink ribbons have been worked together (right) and tied in a multiloop bow.

Combining plain and patterned ribbon can create eye-catching gift wraps. The parcel (left) uses a combination of orange wire-edge ribbon and narrow gingham tied with a multiloop bow.

Patterned ribbon for binding with a sheer multiloop bow (below) produces a delightfully soft effect.

The bold daisy pattern of this wide ribbon (left) needs no more elaborate finish than a center knot. Long ribbon tails give a hint of luxury.

Three types of ribbon have been used for this luxurious parcel (above right). Wide patterned ribbon simply knotted has been used for the binding. The central multiloop bow is a combination of plain wide ribbon and several colors of narrow ribbon.

Two wire-edged ribbons are used here. A purple ribbon tied in a simple knot binds the parcel and a wide pink ribbon is used for a single bow at the center with generous curled tails.

A multiloop bow in sheer striped ribbon topped with stitched roses creates a soft, feminine gift wrap.

The bold effect here is created by the strong patterning of the ribbon which is tied in a loose multiloop bow.

89

CHRISTMAS TREE BOWS

All kinds of bows can be used to decorate a tree either on their own or together with other trimmings.

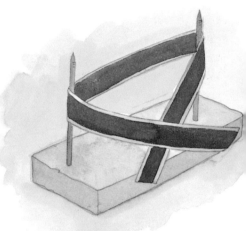

1 Wind ribbon around the nail block, keeping ends of even length. Take care not to injure yourself on the sharp points.

MATERIALS

For each bow you need 28in (70cm) of 1½in (39mm) wire-edge taffeta ribbon.

You can make all your bows in the same color as shown here or use different colors. The bow used for this tree is a single bow made on a 5in (12.5cm) wide nail block.

2 Tie ends at back and round center of bow.

3 Cut ribbon ends into fishtails

4 Attach to tree with florist's wire

A simple picture bow made up in Christmas ribbon is a great way to display your Christmas cards.

This cut edge tartan multiloop bow has a center wire, which makes shaping possible after the bow is formed. A perfect decoration for garlands and extra special gifts.

A wreath bound in tartan and finished with a double loop bow looks pretty on the tree. Alternatively make a pair to adorn each side of the fire place.

A handsome double loop bow in plaid or plain taffeta gives a festive touch to a Christmas table setting or the children's Christmas stockings.

CHRISTMAS BASKET

Decorate a simple basket by weaving ribbon through the side panels. Straight-sided shapes are easiest to work. Add a pretty bow for a finishing touch.

DECORATING THE BASKET

1 Weave the emerald ribbon carefully through the open lattice of the basket, overlapping the ends, and joining them neatly with a dab of glue.

2 Make a large multiloop bow (see page 86) from the remaining emerald ribbon, secure with a long length of binding wire, cut ends of ribbon at an angle.

3 Make similar bows from the other two ribbons. Arrange the bows in your hand one on top of the other, and bind together with the long wire of the cotton bow.

4 Wire the multiloop bow to the inner rim at one end of the basket.

5 Arrange the grasses, flowers, and fruit in position and glue in place.

EASTER BASKET

What better way to present colorful Easter eggs than in this pretty basket you have decorated yourself with satin, lace, and gingham bows.

MATERIALS

Ribbons
- 3¼yd (3m) of ⅞in (23mm) wide yellow singleface satin
- 4¼yd (3.80m) of ⅝in (15mm) wide lace and yellow cut-edge
- 2¾yd (2.40m) of ⅞in (23mm) wide gingham
- 32in (80cm) of ⅝in (15mm) wide lace cut-edge

Other materials
- Basket with handle
- Assorted dried grasses and small flowers

DECORATING THE BASKET

1 Make three bows from the ⅞in (23mm) gingham and a florist's or multiloop bow from 32in (80cm) of the ⅝in (15mm) wide lace cut-edge ribbon.

2 Bind handle with 1¼yd (1m) ⅞in (23mm) singleface satin ribbon, and glue in position at either end.

3 Bind 1¼yd (1m) lace cut-edge over the top of the satin ribbon and glue. Repeat binding around the rim of the basket.

4 Glue small pieces of dried grasses and small flowers along the ribbon edge, carefully hiding the stalks under the ribbon.

5 Attach two gingham bows at either end of handle, and one at the center top of handle.

Layers of looped ribbons cascading down the handle of plain baskets and trimmed with bows or roses at the sides make perfect gift baskets or decorative containers for floral arrangements or for the dressing table.

6

ROSE-MAKING

ROSE-MAKING TECHNIQUES • FESTIVE CENTER PIECE
BRIDAL HEAD PIECE • BRIDE'S BOUQUET • ROSE BALL
WEDDING CENTER PIECE • ROSE-TRIMMED PARCELS

ROSE-MAKING TECHNIQUES

Ribbon roses are incredibly versatile: they can decorate bridal wear, hats, shoes, accessories, and add finishing touches to many other projects.

The width of the ribbon determines the amount you need for making one rose or rosebud. You can make a tiny stitched rose with ¼in (7mm) wide ribbon but anything less than ⅝in (15mm) is too difficult to work with for the stemmed variety. The chart shows how much ribbon you need for each rose according to width. To work two ribbons together, double the amount.

WIDTH OF RIBBON	LENGTH OF RIBBON	
	Stemmed & Stitched Roses	Rosebuds
³⁄₁₆in (5mm)	5in (13cm)	
¼in (7mm)	8in (20cm)	3in (8cm)
⅜in (9mm)	8in (20cm)	3in (8cm)
⅝in (15mm)	16in (40cm)	6in (15cm)
⅞in (23mm)	20in (50cm)	6in (15cm)
1½in (39mm)	32in (80cm)	16in (40cm)
2¼in (56mm)	1½yd (1.25m)	20in (50cm)

BASIC METHODS

For floral arrangements, corsages and gift boxes, the ribbon roses are made on stem wires, but for most fabric projects they are hand stitched. Both versions are basically made in the same way.

TENSION

The tighter you fold and twist the ribbon, the smaller the finished rose will become, so it will look larger, softer, and more open if you work it loosely. By varying the tension of every rose you will create a spray of unique blooms – just as if they had been picked from the garden.

Wire edge ribbons made into bows and roses look great – whether you choose one rose or a cluster of 3 or more. Here, an ombré taffeta rose with lavish tails produces a stylish summer look.

STEMMED ROSE

This rose is made on a wire, so in addition to ribbon you will also need a length of stub wire, some florist's binding wire and floral tape. You can finish off with artificial rose leaves if you like.

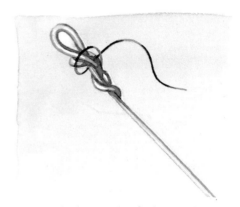

1 Bend the end of the stub wire into a loop. Thread and fasten a piece of binding wire around to secure it.

2 Fold ribbon end over the loop and gather it around stem, tightly winding the binding wire around three times.

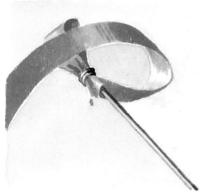

3 Pull end of ribbon up and then out sideways.

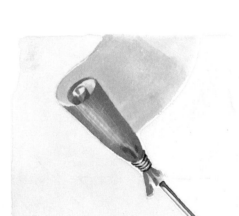

4 Roll the ribbon around four times to form a tight tube and secure with binding wire.

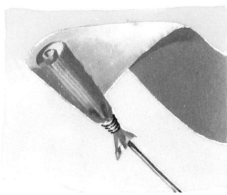

5 Make each petal by first diagonally folding the ribbon end away from you.

6 Turn bud onto center of fold. The bud must always lie inside the rose and come below the edge of the fold. Continue turning bud onto fold until ribbon is straight again, making a cone shape around the bud. Let the binding wire twist itself around the base of the rose as you work, pulling it tight each time you make a petal. Continue making petals until the rose is of the desired size.

7 Bring end of ribbon down to base of rose. Grip it firmly in one hand and wind the binding wire tightly around the base of rose, to secure.

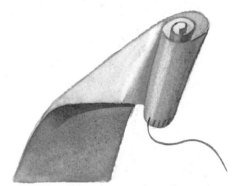

8 Lay the end of the floral tape directly under the rose head and press, stretching it slightly. Turn rose, pressing the tape over the wire to cover it, binding in an artificial leaf if required.

STITCHED ROSE

Whether the roses are made on stem wires or stitched, the process is basically the same. Your only requirement, apart from the ribbon, is a matching thread and a needle.

1 Roll ribbon into a tight tube, making four turns, and stitch bottom of tube to form bud of rose.

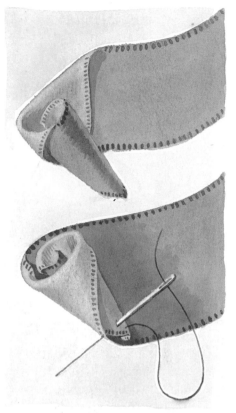

2 Now follow the method for the stemmed rose up to step 7 but stitch the base after each turn instead of binding with wire.

WIRE-EDGE RIBBON ROSE

Lengths of wire-edged taffeta make beautiful cabbage-type roses that give a very different effect from the folded versions.

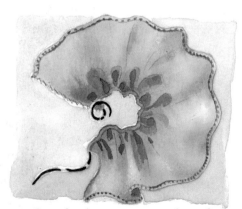

1 Simply draw up one edge of the wire, fastening it at the other end to stop the whole length of wire coming through.

2 Turn in the raw end and gather the ribbon up tightly so that it coils around itself to form a flower shape.

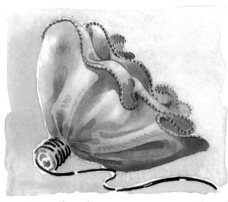

3 Use the drawn up wire to bind the base of the rose, or stitch with needle and thread.

RIBBON ROSETTE

This method of making a rose works particularly well with paper and cut-edge ribbons. It principally involves folding and finally pulling through and twisting, and gives yet another look to our rose collection. Just follow the diagrams below.

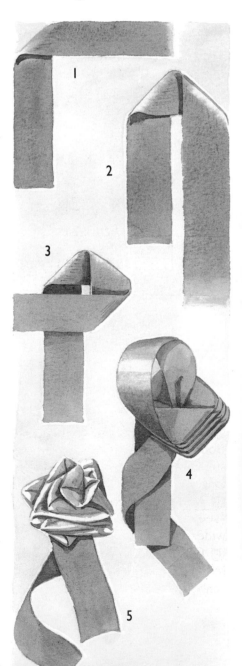

FESTIVE CENTER PIECE

This stylish dinner party decoration shows how a clever choice of ribbon – floral printed metallics – can transform the look of a basic arrangement.

MATERIALS

Ribbons
- 4¾yd (4.20m) of 39mm (1½in) wide metallic
- 2¼yd (2m) of ⅜in (9mm) wide metallic

Other materials
- Gold candle and four cocktail picks
- Seven artificial gold leaves
- Thirty gold baubles
- Six poppy seedheads sprayed gold
- Circle of cardboard approx 5½in (14cm) diameter
- Black felt to cover cardboard
- Small piece florist's foam about 2½in (6cm) diameter by 1¼in (3cm) high

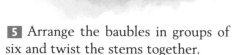

5 Arrange the baubles in groups of six and twist the stems together.

6 Arrange roses, bows, baubles, and other decorations around candle, completely covering foam.

MAKING THE CENTER PIECE

1 Make seven stemmed ribbon roses from 1½in (39mm) wide ribbon. The stems need only be about 2in (5cm) long.

2 Make four wired multiloop bows (see page 86) from ⅜in (9mm) wide ribbon.

3 Cover the cardboard with black felt, and glue the florist's foam to the center.

4 Tape the cocktail sticks to the bottom of the candle and position in center of foam.

This stunning corsage can be worn on an evening dress, attached to a bag or belt, or worn in your hair. It's quickly made by wiring together two multiloop bows, a ribbon rose and a few gold baubles and leaves. You could adapt the idea, choosing your ribbons and baubles to match a favorite outfit.

BRIDAL HEAD PIECE

This pretty circlet of ribbon roses with artificial flowers, pearl beads, ribbon loops, and streamers is perfect for a bride or bridesmaids.

RIBBONS AND BOWS

1 Make four stemmed ribbon roses (see page 96) using the ⅞in (23mm) wide pink taffeta ribbon.

2 Make two multiloop bows with tails (see page 86), one from the 1½in (39mm) wide white ribbon and one from the ⅛in (3mm) wide pink ribbon.

MAKING THE HEAD PIECE

1 Measure the bride's or bridesmaid's head and make a wire ring to fit using several florist's stub wires bound together with floral tape.

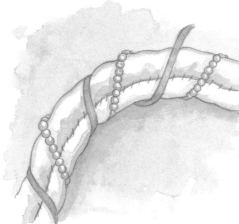

2 Cover the wire ring with batting and then wrap with the doubleface ivory satin ribbon, stitching the ends at the back. Carefully wind the beading and narrow pink ribbon evenly around the ring.

3 Make up two small sprays with the roses and small artificial flowers, covering the stems with floral tape. Stitch and glue the sprays at the back of the head piece leaving a 2½in (6cm) space.

4 Stitch and glue the sheer and narrow ribbons bows together in the center of the space between the flower sprays.

5 Glue a small artificial flower into the center of the bows and trim the tails to length.

BRIDE'S BOUQUET

Choose ribbons in a color combination to suit the occasion, and to ring the changes, add dried, natural or artificial flowers or different ribbons.

MAKING THE BOUQUET

1 Mount the white sheer bows on florist's stub wires and use more floral tape to bind each one to the stem of an ivory rose, about 1¼in (3cm) below the flower.

2 Mount the other bows on shorter lengths of florist's stub wire.

3 Group the roses and sheer bows into a posy in your hand, with some of the larger ones above or below others. Bind together with wire, keeping the binding in one place for a neat finish.

4 Add the smaller roses and flower sprays and bind into position, then bind in the large striped bows at the bottom.

5 To form the handle, cut the stems below the binding to approx 6in (15cm).

6 For a neat finish, bind the two ivory loop taffeta bows in place at the top of the handle under the bouquet.

7 Cover the handle with floral tape and then cover with the ivory taffeta.

This corsage is based on a single stemmed rose, embellished with bows.

ROSES AND BOWS

Make the following stemmed ribbon roses (see page 96). The stems need to be about 10in (25cm) long.

Nine large roses from the 2¼in (56mm) wide cream with gold wire-edge

Ten smaller roses from ⅞in (23mm) wide pink taffeta

Make the following multiloop bows (see page 86):

Five bows from 1½in (39mm) wide white sheer

Three larger bows from 1½in (39mm) wide white sheer with stripes

Two bows from the ⅞in (23mm) wide ivory taffeta

MATERIALS

Ribbons
- 7yd (6.3m) of 2¼in (56mm) wide cream with gold wire-edge
- 5½yd (5m) of ⅞in (23mm) wide pink taffeta
- 5½yd (5m) of 1½in (39mm) wide white sheer
- 5yd (4.5m) of 1½in (39mm) wide white sheer with satin stripes
- 1¼yd (1m) of ⅞in (23mm) wide ivory taffeta

Other materials
- Ten small artificial flower sprays
- Florist's stub wire, binding wire and floral tape

ROSE BALL

A pretty accessory in pink satin ribbon for a bridesmaid to carry. Coordinate the ribbon colours of the dress and head piece for a stunning effect.

MAKING THE BALL

1 Pierce the foam ball through its center with the stub wire, then bend each protruding end of the wire to form a small loop.

2 Cut each of the ⅛in (3mm) wide ribbons in half. Take one length of each shade and slip through one of the stub wire loops then knot ends to form a hanging loop.

3 Next thread the remaining three ribbons through the other stub wire loop on the ball to create a tail, securing them with a pearl-headed pin.

4 Make 72 stitched roses (see page 97) from the six different shades of ⅝in (15mm) ribbon.

5 Divide the ball into six sections and outline with cloves. Place remaining pearl-headed pins equally spaced along each line of cloves. Fill each section with 12 roses of one shade, attaching each one with a pin.

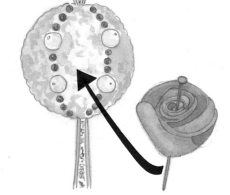

6 Cut the ⅞in (23mm) wide ribbon into four equal lengths and fold and wire each length into a center-bound bow (see page 83). Insert two bows at each end of ball close to tail and close to hanging loop.

7 Make up six stitched roses from ¼in (7mm) ribbon and stitch each one to a contrasting colored ribbon tail. Glue pearl beads to top bow to finish.

WEDDING CENTER PIECE

This romantic arrangement of flowers and ribbons in bridal colors with matching candle is guaranteed to set the festive mood for a great occasion.

MATERIALS

Ribbons

- 6yd (5.4m) of ⅜in (9mm) wide feather-edge green
- 3½yd (3.2m) of ⅞in (23mm) wide white sheer
- 2yd (1.8m) of 1½in (39mm) wide doubleface satin pink
- 2¼yd (2m) of ⅞in (23mm) wide pink taffeta
- 4½yd (4m) of ⅞in (23mm) wide cream taffeta
- 3¼yd (3m) of 1½in (39mm) wide cream sheer

Other materials

- Eight small flower sprays
- One pink candle
- One candle holder or four cocktail picks and clear Scotch tape
- Piece of dry florist's foam or Styrofoam
- 8in (20cm) diameter cake board
- All-purpose glue

ROSES AND BOWS

1 Make the following stemmed ribbon roses:

Three from the 1½in (39mm) wide pink doubleface satin
Four from the ⅞in (23mm) wide pink taffeta
Eight from the ⅞in (23mm) wide cream taffeta
Five from the 1½in (39mm) wide cream sheer

2 Following the instructions on page 86, make nine multiloop bows from the ⅜in (9mm) wide green feather-edge and four from the ⅞in (23mm) white sheer

ASSEMBLING THE CENTER PIECE

1 Glue the dry foam or Styrofoam to the center of the cake board.

2 Position candle in holder or use clear Scotch tape to bind cocktail picks to the base of the candle, position candle in the foam.

3 Arrange the roses and bows around the candle so that the foam is covered.

A single ribbon rose on a long stem makes a simple and elegant napkin ring (left). Choose a color to link in with table decorations. A soft finish is achieved by trimming the satin ribbon with sheer bows and streamers.

103

ROSE-TRIMMED PARCELS

*These prettily decorated parcels are easy to make once you
have mastered the rose making techniques – a lovely way
to make any gift extra special.*

A

B

MATERIALS

Singleface satin ribbon
- 16in (40cm) of ⅛in (3mm) wide pale pink
- 16in (40cm) of ⅛in (3mm) wide pale blue
- 16in (40cm) of ⅛in (3mm) wide cream
- 20in (50cm) of ¼in (7mm) wide pale pink
- 1yd (90cm) of ⅝in (15mm) wide mid-pink
- 1¾yd (1.60m) of ⅞in (23mm) wide deep pink

Sheer stripe ribbon
- 27in (70cm) of 1½in (39mm) wide

Satin printed ribbon
- ⅞in (23mm) wide to wrap the length and width of parcel A
- 1½in (35mm) wide to wrap the length and width of parcel B

Other materials
- Fabric or wrapping paper for the two parcels
- About 12in (30cm) of pearl beading
- Six silk rose leaves
- Florist's wire and floral tape
- Double-sided clear Scotch tape

WRAPPING

Wrap the parcels tightly in the fabric
or paper. Circle the parcels along
their lengths and widths with satin
printed ribbon, sealing the ends
neatly on top with adhesive tape.

PARCEL A

1 Make an assortment of ribbon
roses and rosebuds on fine wire
stems from three of the pink ribbons. Use the whole length of the
¼in (7mm) wide ribbon, a 10in
(25cm) length of the ⅝in (15mm),
and a 30in (75cm) length of the ⅞in
(23mm) ribbon. Do not wrap the
wires in floral tape.

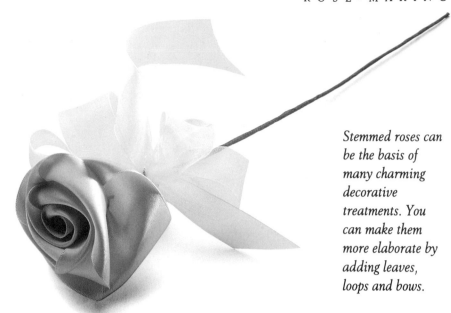

Stemmed roses can be the basis of many charming decorative treatments. You can make them more elaborate by adding leaves, loops and bows.

2 Using the three lengths of ⅛in (3mm) ribbons, wire a ribbon loop as shown in the illustration.

3 Wire the pearl beading into four individual loops. Assemble the roses, leaves and buds in your hand, slip the beading loops in at the back, and

These delightfully unusual parcels are trimmed with stemmed roses and rosebuds, with pearl beading and multiloop bows giving an extra touch of luxury.

bind together with one of the wire stems of a rose. Cover the combined stems with floral tape.

4 Add the ribbon loop below and in front of the largest rose and stick the spray to the parcel.

PARCEL B

1 Make an assortment of five roses and two to three rosebuds on fine wire stems, using the remaining 26in (65cm) of ⅝in (15mm) wide ribbon

and the remaining 34in (85cm) of ⅞in (23mm) ribbon. Do not wrap the wire stems with floral tape.

2 Fold and wire a double bow (see page 83) from sheer stripe ribbon, slanting the ends, and tape it to the top of the parcel.

3 Assemble the roses, leaves, and buds in your hand and bind together with the wire stem of one of the roses, then cover combined stems with stem wrap.

4 Stick the spray to the center of the sheer bow with double-sided Scotch tape.

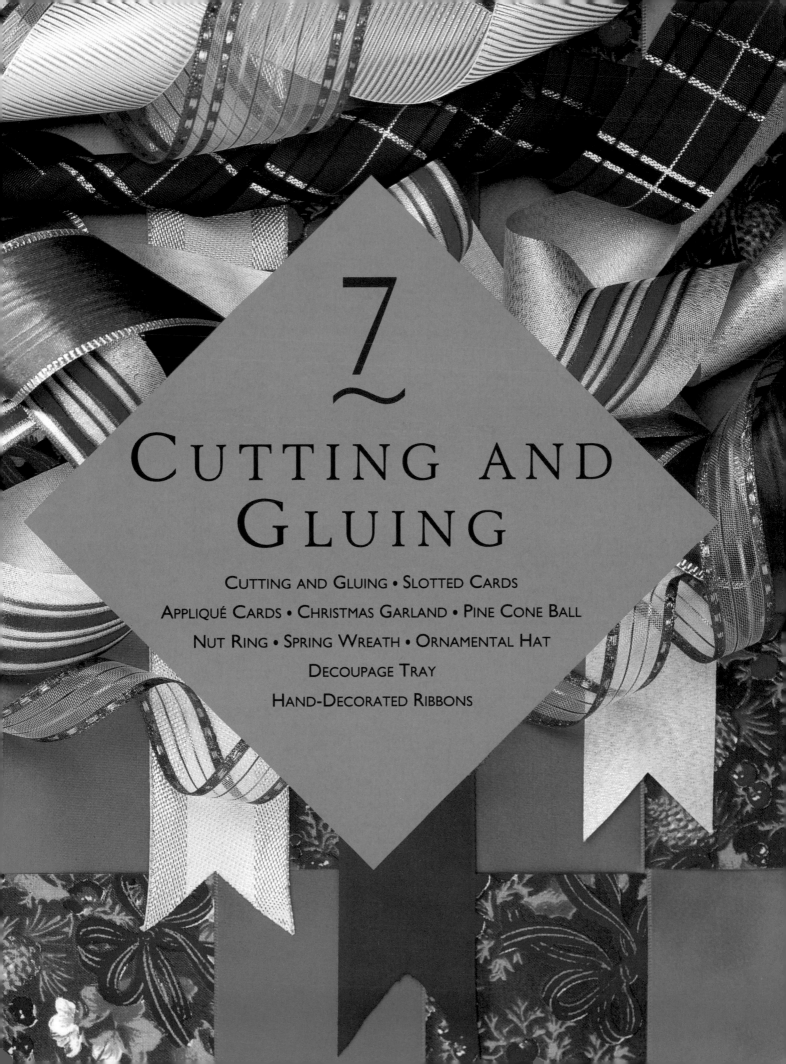

7

CUTTING AND GLUING

CUTTING AND GLUING

Craft (cut-edge) ribbons, available in a multitude of colors and finishes, are ideal for many decorative ribbon projects.

Craft ribbon can be used in the same way as woven-edge ribbon or it can be cut into shapes for making flowers and leaves or used for decoupage. This type of ribbon pleats beautifully and can be splayed into fan shapes.

CRAFT RIBBONS

Craft ribbons and lace, which are treated with special finishes to curb fraying, are generally stiffer than woven-edge ribbons, making them ideal for loops and bows that need to maintain their shape as well as for a host of other craft projects.

Craft ribbons are not washable, so reserve them for projects such as cards and garlands that you don't want to keep forever.

DECOUPAGE

This is another craft for which these ribbons are ideal. Decoupage, whose name comes from the French word *couper*, to cut, was a very popular craft in Victorian times. All kinds of wooden surfaces were covered in cut-out illustrations, which were then given several layers of varnish.

Craft ribbons lend themselves perfectly to this hobby, as they are just as easy to cut and glue down as pieces of paper. If you use ribbons with a printed pattern you can cut a variety of motifs and borders, and the ribbon won't fray because of the special fabric finish.

The best way to work is to cut a variety of motifs and then move them around on your chosen surface until a design begins to "gel." Don't be afraid to overlap cuttings for effect, or to turn a motif into something different. For example, you could cut a large flower into the shape of an egg.

GLUE GUNS

These are very useful for projects where some bonding is required, such as greeting cards, decoupage items, decorated baskets, and floral decorations. There are various different types on the market, some being "hot melt" and others "low melt." Whichever you choose always follow the manufacturer's instructions, and be sure to keep the gun out of the reach of children. Always hold the glued parts for several seconds to make sure the bond is strong.

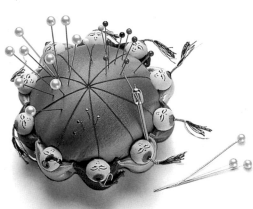

A selection of pins in differing lengths are useful for securing roses and bows to displays.

Glue guns are ideal for building up arrangements by bonding ribbons and dried flowers to wreaths and similar decorative items.

A variety of wires, both thick and thin, are essential for many craft projects involving cut and glued ribbon.

Fruits and berries are a clever way to introduce additional shape, color and texture.

Wire cutters are a must for frequent users of stem and binding wires in craft projects.

FLORIST'S WIRE AND TAPE

A variety of wires and tapes are available from florists, gardening, and craft shops and are used for various projects in this chapter. A sturdy but bendable wire is ideal for making stems for ribbon roses and bows and heavier dried flower heads and cones. This is often referred to as stem wire, and usually comes ready cut into lengths of between 6in (15cm) and 12in (30cm).

A finer wire is needed to fix a stem wire to the ribbon rose or other flower. It is also useful for securing the centers of bows and for attaching bows, roses, and flowers and so on to floral wreaths, topiaries etc. Binding wire is made in a medium to fine gauge and is usually available by the reel.

Stemmed ribbon roses are enhanced with an artificial leaf or two. Smaller leaves are best with narrow ribbons.

Always cut craft wire with wire-cutters or old scissors, as it will ruin good fabric scissors.

You will also need floral tape to bind wire stems and to attach leaves or other flowers. The wax tape sticks to itself and gives a smooth finish. It is sold by the reel and is usually green, although other colors are available in some stores.

A waxy, sticky tape for binding stems is available in green or brown.

A variety of bases are available for designing garlands, wreaths, posies and other arrangements.

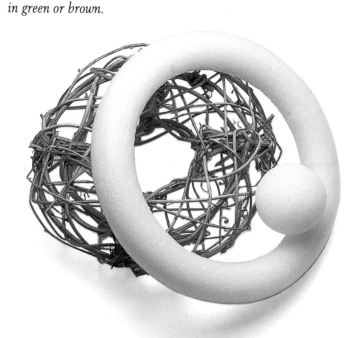

When using dried flowers as a general rule limit yourself to three colors excluding your main color.

SLOTTED CARDS

*A deceptively simple way to decorate a greeting card
or gift tag, all you need is a craft knife, a cutting
board, a ruler, pencil, and glue.*

CHRISTMAS TREE
CARD AND GIFT TAG

MATERIALS

Craft ribbons – all ⅞in (23mm) wide
- 8¾in (22cm) green
- 3¼in (8cm) taffeta plaid
- 3¼in (8cm) red
- 1¾in (4cm) sheer
- 2¼in (6cm) light green
- 2in (5cm) swiss dot red

Doubleface satin ribbon – all ⅛in
(3mm) wide
- 10in (25cm) mini-dot red
- 5in (13cm) white
- 1½yd (1.40m) red
- 15¾in (40cm) emerald green
- 5in (13cm) dark green

Other materials
- Piece of Bristol board 16in by 6½in
  (40.5cm by 16.5cm)
- Piece of Bristol board 10½in by 1½in
  (27cm by 3.5cm)
- Clear all-purpose glue

MAKING THE CARD

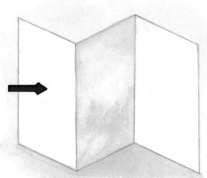

MAKING THE CARD

1 Score and fold the large piece of Bristol board into three as shown.

2 Trace the pattern onto the front section of the card, then cut the slots making sure they are cut cleanly to the edge.

3 Thread ribbon through slots, securing at the back with glue.

4 Thread the red ⅛in (3mm) ribbon in and out of the slots at the edges so that the longest pieces show on the front.

5 Tie bows at corners, glue tails into position, and glue first two folds of card together to finish.

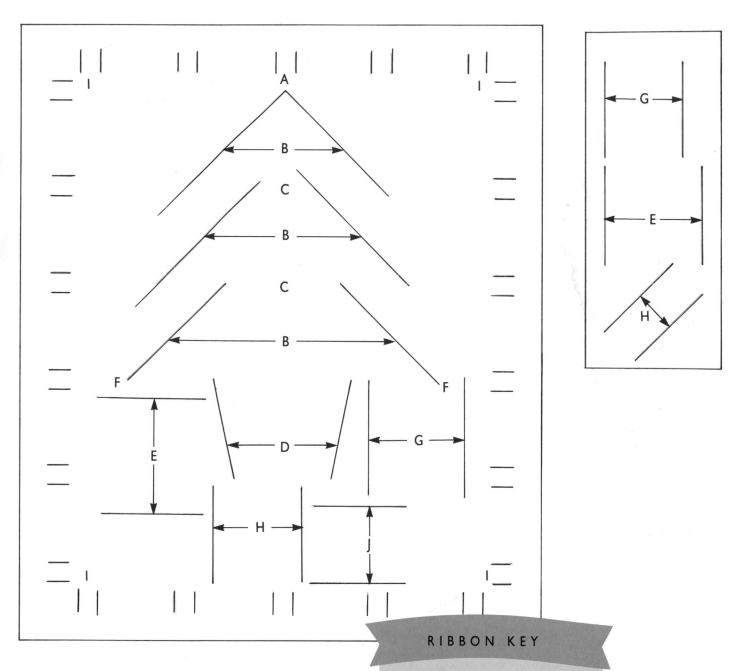

MAKING THE GIFT TAG
1 Score and fold remaining Bristol board into three 3½in (9cm) folds as before.
2 Cut slots, decorate with ribbon and finish as before.

RIBBON KEY

A = Silver star
B = Green and gold
C = Mini-dot red bow
D = Swiss dot red
E = Taffeta plaid
F = Emerald green bow
G = Red
H = Light green
I = Red bow
J = Sheer

METALLIC STAR

MATERIALS

For the card
- Piece of navy Bristol board 6in (15cm) square
- Piece of white Bristol board 6¼in by 12½in (16cm by 32cm)
- 24in (60cm) of ⅞in (23mm) wide metallic ribbon.

For the tag
- Piece of blue Bristol board 1½in by 2¾in (4cm by 7cm)
- Piece of white Bristol board 1½in by 2¾in (4cm by 7cm)
- 14in (35cm) of ⅛in (3mm) wide grosgrain ribbon
- 2¼in (5½cm) of ⅞in (23mm) wide metallic ribbon

MAKING THE STAR

1 Enlarge the pattern opposite and trace it onto the navy Bristol board, then cut slots and thread ribbon horizontally.

2 Glue ends in place on reverse side and cut through ribbons at center.

3 Fold and carefully glue each cut end back on itself to expose the other center slots.

4 Thread vertical ribbons through, and glue ends in place on reverse side.

5 Score down center of the white card and fold in half.

6 Mount navy Bristol board onto the front of white Bristol board and color border with a gold pen.

MAKING THE GIFT TAG

1 Following the diagram above, cut windows out of blue Bristol board.

112

Scale 1 square = ⁵⁄₁₆in (8mm)

A panel of woven ribbon over which a window in the shape of your chosen design has been placed, is a quick way to make a pretty card. Zig-zag weave (above) makes an effective Christmas tree design.

2 Glue vertical pieces of ribbon in place as shown, then weave and glue the horizontal ribbons.

3 Mount the blue Bristol board on white Bristol board onto which the ⅞in (23mm) metallic ribbon has been glued.

For a three-dimensional effect, place batting under your woven panel. The Valentine's day card (right) also uses appliquéd lace ribbon to add to its romantic appeal.

Appliqué Cards

Using highly versatile craft ribbon, individual handmade gift and greeting cards are fun to design and wonderful to receive, and need not be time-consuming to make.

WEDDING CARD AND GIFT TAG

MATERIALS

Ribbons
- 11in (27cm) of 2¼in (56mm) wide silver craft
- 1¾yd (1.50m) of ¹⁄₁₆in (1.5mm) wide white
- Four small ribbon roses

Other materials
- Square of net 4¾in (12cm)
- White Bristol board 7in by 11in (18cm by 28cm)
- Pale blue Bristol board 7in by 5½in (18cm by 14cm)
- Pale colored paper 7in by 5½in (18cm by 14cm)
- White Bristol board 7in by 11in (18cm by 28cm)
- White Bristol board 4½in by 2¼in (11cm by 5.6cm) for the tag

4 Glue the net behind this window, then glue the paper window onto the blue card.

MAKING THE CARD
1 Score down center of white Bristol board and fold in half.
2 Stick the pale blue Bristol board over front of Bristol board.
3 Cut out a 4in (10cm) square from the center of the pale pastel paper to make a window.

MAKING THE BELL

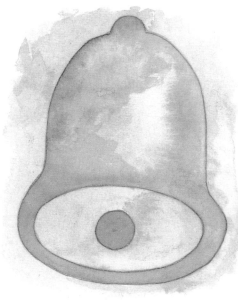

1 Trace the bell shape and make a template, then cut two bells from the wide silver craft ribbon.
2 Glue bells on net and dress with three ribbon roses and about 1¼yd (1m) of white ribbon, following the photograph.

MAKING THE TAG
1 Cover the 4½in by 2¼in (11cm by 5.6cm) card with silver craft ribbon and fold in half.
2 Dress with white ribbon and a ribbon rose, punch a hole in the corner and thread with 5in (13cm) of white ribbon.

3 Make the half flowers in the same way, but after stitching and opening out the first fan, glue only from the center to one outside edge, then adjust the pleats to form a semi-circle.

4 To make foliage curls cut eight 4in (10cm) lengths of the ⅜in (9mm) wide green ribbon. Roll each length tightly and glue at base to create four double curls.

MAKING THE CARD

1 Score down center of eight 7in by 14in (18cm by 36cm) card and fold in half.

2 From the contrast card cut out center to leave a ½in (13mm) border all round. Stick to front of card.

3 Glue four full flowers, three half flowers and three foliage curls in place.

MAKING THE TAG

1 Cover the 5in by 1½in (13cm by 3.9cm) card with craft ribbon.

2 Score card, fold in half and glue a half flower and foliage curl to the front, following the photograph.

3 Punch a hole in one corner, and thread with 5in (13cm) length of ¹⁄₁₆in (1.5mm) wide ribbon.

BIRTHDAY CARD AND GIFT TAG

MATERIALS

Ribbons
- 7in (18cm) of 1½in (39mm) wide craft in two different floral prints; 4in (10cm) in a third print
- 32in (80cm) of ⅜in (9mm) wide craft in pale green
- 5in (13cm) of ¹⁄₁₆in (1.5mm) wide blue ribbon

Other materials
- Bristol board 7in by 14in (18cm by 36cm)
- Bristol board 7in (18cm) square in contrasting color
- Bristol board 5in by 1½in (13cm by 3.9cm)
- Sewing thread

MAKING THE FLOWERS AND FOLIAGE

Using 1½in (39mm) wide craft ribbon, make four full and four half flowers as follows. Each full flower needs approximately 4in (10cm) of ribbon, and each half flower approximately 2¾in (7cm) of ribbon.

1 For the full flowers, fold the ribbon concertina-fashion every ¼in (7mm), stitch through center, pull tight and secure.

2 Open out one side into a fan, glue end fold to the end fold of the other half, then open out other side; sew a sequin in center.

115

CHRISTMAS WREATH
CARD AND TAG

MATERIALS

- 11in (28cm) of 1¼in (32mm) wide craft ribbon in Christmas colors
- Ribbon bow
- White Bristol board 7in by 11in (18cm by 28cm)
- Red Bristol board 7in by 5½in (18cm by 14cm)
- White Bristol board 5in by 1¼in (13cm by 3.2cm)
- Small piece of 1¼in (32mm) craft ribbon in color to blend with bow
- 5in (13cm) of ¹⁄₁₆in (1.5mm) ribbon

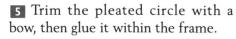

MAKING THE CARD

1 Score down center of white Bristol board and fold in half.

2 Cut a 4in (10cm) square window in middle of red Bristol board and glue to the white Bristol board.

3 Make ¼in (6mm) pleats in ribbon and stitch through near base.

4 Pull up thread and secure, then make into a circle by opening out pleats and gluing ends together.

5 Trim the pleated circle with a bow, then glue it within the frame.

MAKING THE TAG

1 Cover one side of the Bristol board with craft ribbon.

2 Score and fold Bristol board down center, cutting a V in the ends of the Bristol board to look like bow tails.

3 Punch a hole in corner of the Bristol board and thread with the ¹⁄₁₆in (1.5mm) ribbon.

CHRISTMAS GARLAND

Traditional tartans, stripes, and festive green and red ribbons are the basis for this sumptuous garland, ideal for placing along a mantelpiece or banister rail.

MATERIALS

Ribbons
- 1¾yd (1.50m) of 1½in (39mm) wide cut-edge velour green
- 1¾yd (1.50m) of 1½in (39mm) wide cut-edge tartan
- 3¼yd (2.90m) of 1½in (39mm) wide cut-edge red/green/gold
- 5½yd (5m) of ⅞in (23mm) wide cut-edge tartan

Other materials
- 1½yd (1.30m) twisted vine
- 4⅓yd (4m) gold beading
- Eight small sprays artificial berries
- Twenty pine cones sprayed gold
- Florist's stub wire and glue

MAKING THE GARLAND

1 Cut the cut-edge red/green/gold into two 27in (70cm) lengths. Cut each piece lengthwise into three and make six multiloop bows (see page 86) mounted on florist's stub wire.

2 From the ⅞in (23mm) tartan cut-edge make ten multiloop bows mounted on florist's wire.

3 Mount the sprayed pine cones on stub wire and bind the gold beading around the whole length of the vine.

4 Mark the center point of the vine and arrange all the berries, cones and bows along the length, pushing the wires into the vine and glueing to secure.

5 Make three large multiloop bows with tails from three 1¾yd (1.50m) lengths of the 1½in (39mm) wide ribbon, and put them together to form one large bow.

6 Position this bow in the center of the vine, glue in place, and trim tails to desired length.

PINE CONE BALL

Pretty enough to use singly, or in a group, decorated cone balls look attractive suspended from the ceiling at different heights, rather like chime bells.

MAKING THE BALL

1 Pierce the foam ball through its center with the stub wire, bending each end to form a small loop close to the ball. Trim off any excess.

2 Cut two 8in (20cm) lengths of the ⅞in (23mm) wide sand ribbon and use binding wire to make two double loops.

3 Make six stitched ribbon roses (see page 97) with the remaining sand ribbon, and another two loops and six roses from the ⅞in (23mm) wide light brown ribbon.

4 Cut six 6in (15cm) lengths of gold ribbon and use binding wire to make six double loops.

5 From the remaining gold ribbon make three stitched ribbon roses.

6 Set aside two 24in (60cm) lengths of ⅝in (15mm) wide satin print ribbon, then use wire to make fourteen double loops from the remaining printed ribbon.

MATERIALS

Ribbons
- 2yd (1.80m) of ⅞in (23mm) satin sand
- 2½yd (2.25m) of ⅝in (15mm) wide satin gold
- 2yd (1.80m) of ⅞in (23mm) wide acetate light brown
- 24in (60cm) of ⅝in (15mm) wide acetate light brown
- 4yd (3.40m) of ⅝in (15mm) wide satin print

Other materials
- Ball of dry florist's foam 4in (10cm) diameter
- About 36 small pine cones
- Binding wire
- 6in (15cm) length of stub wire
- Clear all-purpose adhesive

7 Make four wired double loops from the light brown ⅝in (15mm) wide ribbon.

8 Thread one 24in (60cm) length of printed ribbon through the wire loop on one side of the ball, and stitch or knot the ends together to form a hanging loop.

9 Thread the remaining printed ribbon and gold ribbon together through the opposite stub wire loop to form the lower tail.

10 Cover the ball with prepared roses, loops, and pine cones, pinning or gluing them in place.

NUT RING

*For a delightful center piece for the Christmas table, make
a traditional nut ring and add colorful ribbons to contrast
with the natural dark brown tones.*

MAKING THE RING

1 Divide the nuts, pods, and cones into four equal groups.

2 At the 3, 6, 9, and 12 o'clock positions on the ring, wire or glue the groups of nuts, pods and cones, leaving a gap of 2in (5cm) between the adjacent groups; spray with varnish.

3 Cut four 3in (7.5cm) lengths of velvet ribbon. Fishtail one end of each piece and make a pleat and stitch in place at the other.

4 Glue the stitched end flat to the ring between each group of nuts with the "fishtail" protruding outwards.

MATERIALS

Ribbons
- 24in (60cm) of 2¾in (68mm) wide velvet burgundy
- 4yd (3.90m) of 1½in (39mm) wide plaid
- 2yd (1.80m) of ⅞in (23mm) wide metallic nylon copper

Other materials
- Vine ring approx 9in (23cm) diameter
- 1lb (450gm) of assorted nuts
- 8 jacaranda pods or similar
- 4 larch cones or similar
- 12 macrocarpa cones or similar
- Binding wire
- Clear varnish
- Clear all-purpose glue

5 Cut the plaid ribbon into four, fold and wire each piece into a triple folded bow, fishtail the ends, and glue or wire on top of each velvet tail.

6 Cut the metallic ribbon into four, fold and wire each one into a double folded bow, cut the ends at a slant, glue or wire one to the side of each plaid bow.

7 Cut four pieces of velvet ribbon 3in (7.5cm) long and cut them all in half lengthwise. Fishtail one end of each piece and stitch a pleat at the other. Glue two tails between the loops of each plaid bow.

SPRING WREATH

*Celebrate spring with a wreath decorated with bright
colored ribbons and flowers. Suspend it from a ceiling or,
without hanging ribbons, on a door or wall.*

(see page 86)

MATERIALS

Ribbons
- 6½yd (6m) of ⅞in (23mm) wide singleface, yellow
- 5yd (4.50m) of ⅞in (23mm) wide wire-edge, pale yellow

Other materials
- Twisted twig wreath
- Dried flowers and grasses

MAKING THE WREATH

1 Cut the singleface satin ribbon in half. Make the hanging ribbons by cutting one 3¼yd (3m) piece into three equal lengths and attaching them at equal spaces to the wreath.

2 Glue the flowers and grasses around the wreath.

3 Using the wire-edge ribbon, make three multiloop bows (see page 86), and glue one at the base of each hanging ribbon.

4 From the remaining singleface satin ribbon, make a multiloop satin bow and glue to the wreath below the point where the hanging ribbon is attached.

ORNAMENTAL HAT

Bring back memories of sunny summer days with a decorative straw hat to hang on the wall. Select your ribbons and dried flowers to complement your room.

MAKING THE DECORATIONS

1 Make ten multiloop bows (see page 86) from the lace ribbon, nine from the gingham, three from 2yd (1.80m) of cut-edge floral ribbon, and one large multiloop bow with tails from the remaining floral ribbon.

2 Attach a short length of ribbon or string inside the hat for hanging.

3 Place hat flat on a table and glue all the pieces in place, fixing the large multiloop bow to the bottom of the hat, with a small gingham bow in the center.

MATERIALS

Ribbons
- 5½yd (5m) of ⅝in (15mm) wide lace
- 5yd (4.50m) of ⅝in (15mm) wide gingham
- 4⅓yd (4m) of 1½in (39mm) wide cut-edge floral

Other materials
- Large straw hat
- Assorted dried flowers, grasses, and artificial flower sprays
- Small piece of ribbon or string

DECOUPAGE TRAY

Craft ribbons lend themselves well to decoupage; you can cut a variety of borders and motifs, and the ribbon won't fray because of the special fabric finish.

1 Prepare the surface of the tray by either stripping off existing varnish or painting the central panel. You need a clean grease-free surface for the decoupage.

2 Cut the pieces of border ribbon to fit, and glue them on, leaving a small margin at the outer edges.

3 Carefully cut out motifs and shapes that appeal to you and arrange them on the tray. Cut out flowers singly, and overlap your cuttings for an interesting effect.

4 When you are satisfied with your design, glue the shapes into place.

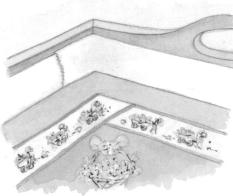

5 Use masking tape to mask any areas that you need to protect from varnish, such as the edges of the tray, then apply a thin coat of varnish and leave to dry.

6 Continue to apply further thin coats of varnish, leaving each one to

MATERIALS

- Craft ribbon – sufficient wide print with repeating pattern to make a border, plus floral prints for individual motifs
- Paper glue
- Wooden tray
- Paint and brushes
- Clear polyurethane varnish
- Sandpaper

dry first, until the cuttings have a glazed appearance. You will need about 15 coats.

7 Rub down the varnish with fine sandpaper, wipe off the dust and apply the final coat of varnish, then remove any masking tape, using a knife to free the edges if necessary.

HAND-DECORATED RIBBONS

Customize accessories for home, work, and school by embellishing ribbons with fabric paints, beads, sequins, stencils, and other decorative findings.

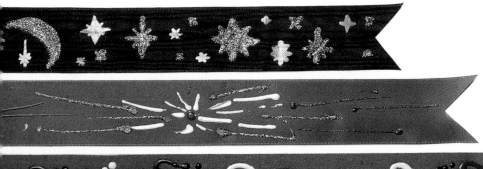

Create your own fireworks with interesting combinations of glitter paints, gold paint, and plastic paint.

FABRIC PAINTS

There are many types of fabric paint available giving a variety of surface effects: raised or flat, shiny, glittery, matt, or metallic. Try splattering paint on ribbon, or apply a stencil using a special stubby stencil brush. Stencils look best on smooth satins in light colors to make lovely trims for home furnishings. Paint ribbons on a flat surface before making them into bows etc. Experiment techniques on spare ribbon first, follow manufacturers' instructions carefully, and always test for color-fastness for use on washable items.

BEADS, PEARLS, SEQUINS, BUTTONS

Decorative jewelry findings, sequins and buttons look superb on ribbon. Either handstitch them or choose a fabric paint which doubles as a glue. Decorate bows or rosettes after you have made them and choose small, lightweight embellishments so the ribbon is not weighed down. Washing can damage the beads or they might come off altogether, so make sure that ribbon can be removed for laundering if necessary.

SPRAY PAINTING

For a completely coordinated look make bows and roses in any left-over ribbons to create a table arrangement or tree decoration along with baubles and artificial or dried flowers, then give the whole lot a couple of coats of spray paint.

Gold, silver, or bronze works well for Christmas, and as the paint stiffens the ribbon, even a single rose or bow in a fine sheer ribbon makes a dramatic and unusual trim for a parcel or Christmas tree.

Use a paint brush and add a touch of water to the fabric paint to produce an artistic watercolor effect. Generally the more dilute the paint, the softer the finished texture.

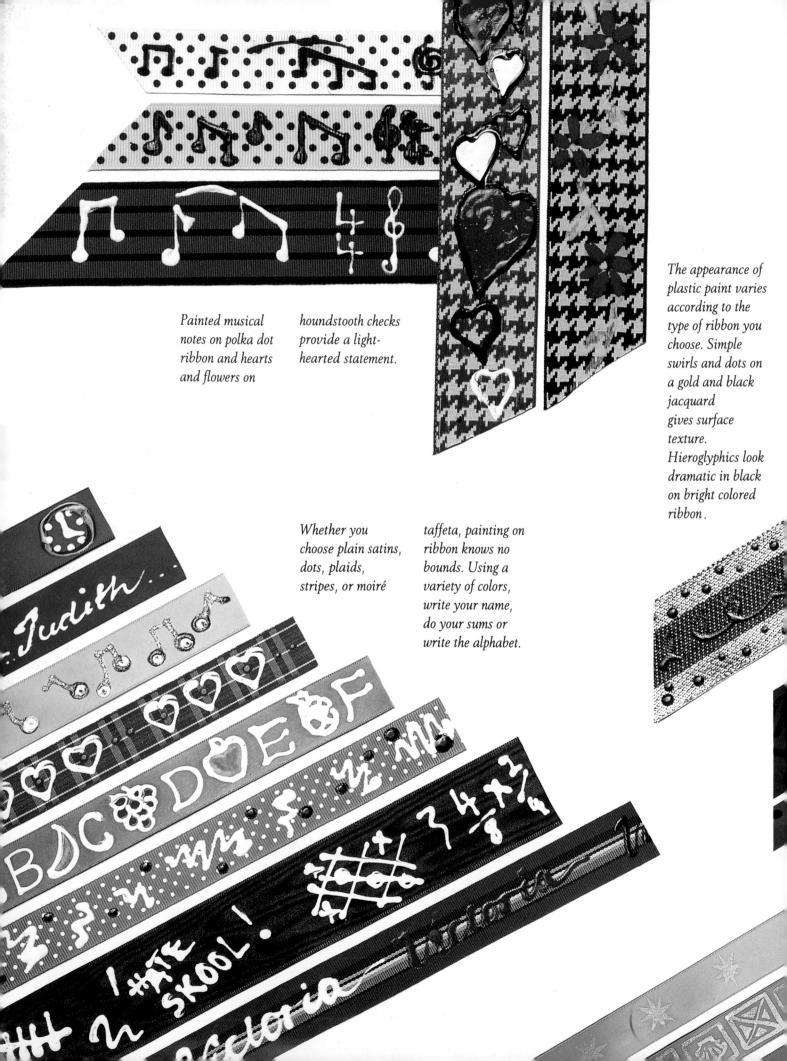

Painted musical notes on polka dot ribbon and hearts and flowers on houndstooth checks provide a light-hearted statement.

The appearance of plastic paint varies according to the type of ribbon you choose. Simple swirls and dots on a gold and black jacquard gives surface texture. Hieroglyphics look dramatic in black on bright colored ribbon.

Whether you choose plain satins, dots, plaids, stripes, or moiré taffeta, painting on ribbon knows no bounds. Using a variety of colors, write your name, do your sums or write the alphabet.

A glitter paint pen has been used to draw around the outline of a pretty floral printed ribbon (left). This technique can be used to highlight interesting motifs and details.

Plastic-look fabric paint (above) is available in primary fluorescent glitter or pearlized colors and is great for creating surface texture. To attach sequins, beads, bows, or diamanté, just squeeze a blob onto the ribbon from the bottle and place the item gently on the paint.

Create all kinds of pop art effects and enjoy the freedom of paint experimentation on ribbon (below). The golden rule is to keep the design simple.

Gold fabric paint produces a rich, oriental look (left).

INDEX

Page references in *italic* type refer to pictures and captions.

CREDITS

Quarto would like to thank C.M. Offray and Lion Ribbon for supplying the ribbon for the projects in this book. Thanks are also due to Anna French for fabrics, Güterman for thread and sewing notions, Newey Goodman for haberdashery, and Vilene for interacing.

The ribbon projects in this book were designed and made by:

Jenny Banham (Neck roll pillow, Woven-square quilt, Wall organizer, Pot pourri sachets, Ruffled cushion, Piped pillow, Log-cabin quilt, Bed linen, Appliqué belts, Evening bag, Child's dress and bag, Pillow trims)

Caroline Birkett-Harris (Table runner, Place mat and coaster, Picture frame, Embroidered card, Christmas table linen, Make-up bag, Sampler panel, Picture bow, Slotted cards, Decoupage tray)

Cathryn Brooker (Easter basket, Festive centerpiece, Bridal Head-piece, Bride's bouquet, Wedding center piece, Christmas garland, Spring wreath, Ornamental hat)

Barbara Carpenter (Bows and gift baskets)

Lindsay Chalford-Brown (Hand-decorated ribbons)

Myra Davidson (Trimmed towels, Curtain tie-backs)

Esme House (Rosettes)

Mary Straka (Christmas basket, Rose ball, Rose-trimmed parcels, Pine ball, Nut ring)

Linda Woods (Embroidered pillow)

Additional samples are by the author.

I would like to give my special thanks to my family for their help and support during the preparation of this book.
                    Christine Kingdom.